Living with
Faith
and
Mental Illness

Tara Taylor

This book is not intended to provide therapy, counseling, or medical treatment or to take the place of clinical advice and treatment from your physician or mental health provider. Readers are advised to consult their personal physician and mental health provider regarding mental health and medical issues.

Living with Faith and Mental Illness

ISBN-13: 978-1544996127

Edited by: Hattie P. Wadlington

Cover and Interior design: JaLana Sheree Walsh, www.favoredimagedesign.com

Cover photography: Adriana Sans

Tara Taylor

www.tarataylor.org

Live Free Church

1911 Grayson Hwy, Ste 8-323 | Grayson, GA 30017 | www.livefreechurch.org

DEDICATION

This book is dedicated to those who struggle with mental health issues.

You may feel alone in your struggle, but remember God knows you and sees you. May this book offer reassurance that you are not alone and you are not forgotten. I pray you have the courage to fight for your life and purpose.

You are worth it!

Isaiah 49:15-16 (NKJV) "Can a woman forget her nursing child, and not have compassion on the son of her womb? Surely they may forget, yet I will not forget you. See, I have inscribed you on the palms of My hands."

ACKNOWLEDGMENTS

Special thanks...

To Terrell, the love of my life. You have been my greatest encourager!

To Mom and Dad Wadlington, for loving me unconditionally.

To Mom and Dad Taylor, for giving of yourself so unselfishly.

To Pastors James and Marie Daniel for constantly pouring the Word of God into me since I was three years old. I was truly able to follow you as you followed Christ.

To Andre'a McElroy, for being my sister and confidante.

To Emely Vazquez, for being my best friend since 8th grade and lovingly putting up with me.

To Sabrina Reynolds, for being a listening ear.

To Ronda Mwangi, for showing me it is okay to laugh at myself.

To Nicole Obialo, for providing me with a quiet space to write.

To Angela Oglesby, for being my prayer partner.

To JaLana Walsh, for your creativity with the process of putting this book together.

To La Shunda Singleton, for your steady friendship.

To Carmen McLean, for support as I embarked on this writing journey.

To Trish Blackwell, for being my amazing life coach.

To Adriana Sans, for serving God with your beautiful gift of photography.

To Marcia McWhorter, for your faithful mentorship.

To Jeanne Mayo, for speaking the truth in love. It was life-changing for me!

To my Live Free Church family, for your many prayers, love and support.

PRAISE FOR
LIVING WITH FAITH AND MENTAL ILLNESS

Tara Taylor's authentic vulnerability in *Living with Faith and Mental Illness* is not only beautiful and enlightening, but it is powerful. This book is a must-have tool for anyone who knows anyone with mental illness, whether it is the reader themselves or someone the reader loves. Tara excels at painting the real picture of what having bipolar feels like, and paired with her foundation in ministry and her experience as a licensed counselor, her words welcome readers to a safe place of hope and healing. I am delighted that Tara is so bold with her writing, as she is unveiling a topic that many struggle to share about, particularly in regards to the relationship between illness and faith. *Living with Faith and Mental Illness* is written from the heart, like you are hearing from a friend, but also from a point of expertise, like you are sitting with a counselor, truly giving you the best of both perspectives and allowing you to feel connected and filled with hope each page of your read.

Trish Blackwell
Confidence Coach, Author, Entrepreneur, Personal Trainer, NASM-CPT
www.trishblackwell.com

The disease of mental illness is real! Tara candidly shares her journey with her diagnosis with bipolar disorder. As I read the pages of this book, it was clear that her desire was to help others in the Body of Christ who have been in bondage in their plight with how to address mental illness. She strives to encourage them to not be afraid or ashamed to seek help. She also challenges us in the body of Christ to look at positive ways to address this issue. Her story is also a source of inspiration, particularly to women who are trying to keep it all together! When you read this book you will gain both spiritual and practical principles from her story. From reading *Living with Faith and Mental Illness* I am committed to not looking at mental illness as a stigma but an illness that requires medical attention, just as many other health issues. I am honored to know Tara as the Christian woman she is today.

Yolanda T. Lee
First Lady, Berean Christian Church

Christians dealing with mental health challenges have too few examples of other Christians who speak openly about how to build a life in community with a sense of purpose and confidence. Because of the stigma associated with mental illness as well as religious ideology that speaks to afflictions as consequences of personal sin and instantaneous healing as the only means by which Christians can be made whole, many Christians are fearful to acknowledge this battle and seek necessary support. *Living with Faith and Mental Illness* speaks to the ability of Christians to be able to move from an either/or mentality to a both/and perspective about faith and mental health… meaning, we can both be people of great faith and patiently take part in a process of healing. It sheds a holistic light on what it means to live truthfully and walk freely as God's own in spite of and because of our struggles. It is a great tool for any person or faith-based congregation to begin and sustain intelligent and life-giving conversations about mental illness, our faith, our ongoing healing, and our need to view self-care as sacred.

Sherria Taylor, PhD, CFLE
Assistant Professor of Child & Family Studies
San Francisco State University

In her book, *Living with Faith and Mental Illness*, Tara beautifully approaches the taboo subject of Mental Health and Christianity. With her real and honest approach, Tara shows that being diagnosed with a Mental Health Disorder doesn't mean you have failed as a Christian. This is a bold and powerful book that can be a game changer for other Christians and their loved ones that struggle with this very relevant issue. A practical tool that is a must have for clinicians, pastors, pastoral counselors, and anyone who needs encouragement and a go-to-handbook on Mental Health.

Brenda Coomer Black, MAMFT, LPC
Hope Forward Counseling & Life Coaching
www.hopeforward.com

Living with Faith and Mental Illness provides an honest and fresh perspective on a much-needed topic—mental health. Tara is able to draw from her clinical expertise and the personal vulnerabilities of her own testimony to provide insight and understanding into the complexities of bipolar disorder and depression. In the process, she beautifully demonstrates how God's love reaches into the dark corners of our soul to bring health and healing through a variety of means. This book will not only benefit greatly those who are struggling in these areas, but will also provide immense comfort and assistance to the loved ones who struggle along with them.

Carmen McLean
Christian Author and
President of Living Above
www.livingabove.net

This story reminds me of God's unceasing love in life's struggles. Hopefully this book will encourage others who have mental illness to seek help and guidance and counsel from Christian counselors and physicians. Be strong, be courageous and trust in the Lord. He is in control of your life if you let him.

Dr. Benjamin Abraham, D.O.
Abraham Medical Cosmetics

This is a must read book that is full of insight and a heart touching victory. I started reading it and could not put it down. You do not have to have a Mental Health challenge to appreciate this book and for it to give you insight and a perspective that gives you hope.

Candi Stewart
Executive Pastor
International Family Worship Center
www.Intlfwc.org

Tara's story inspires hope and provides answers to Believers that hide in the shame of mental illness.

Chris Singleton
Former Major League baseball player

What an impactful book! Living with Faith and Mental Illness is a must-read for those (specifically in the church) dealing with the tension between their "faith" and mental illness. Tara does a powerful job in enlightening the reader about several of the issues connected to mental illness that many of us need to be aware of. Her personal battle and victory in this area brings hope and confidence to all who read. I highly recommend, Living with Faith and Mental Illness for everyone. It is both educational and inspirational and will leave the reader with a confident resolve that there is both Hope and Freedom for those dealing with this sensitive issue.

Chauncey Fourte'
Senior Pastor of Impact Life Centre
Co-Founder of Fourte Coaching
www.impactlifecentre.org | www.fourtecoaching.com

On rare occasions you read material about mental health and feel motivated, hopeful and excited about the future. Living with Faith and Mental Illness gives a genuine, authentic look into Tara's journey with such power to rescue those who feel hopeless. This book celebrates the faithfulness of God in the journey of ones facing mental health issues and the appreciation of seeking healing through medicine and God's Word. I highly recommend this book for all health professionals and those battling with mental health illness.

Gwendolyn Fourte'
Co-Pastor of Impact Life Centre
Co-Founder of Fourte Coaching
www.impactlifecentre.org | www.fourtecoaching.com

Tara shares candidly from her own past about her diagnosis of bipolar disorder and offers insight and advice to those struggling with mental illness and their family members. She does this in an easy to read manner from a Christian counselor's perspective including guidelines from God's word to help those who suffer from mental illness. I believe the simple and easily understandable truths offer hope to those who have misconceptions or feel a stigma from their own diagnosis. It is a concise effort that fulfills a need in the Christian community.

Dr. Patricia Barrington, D.O.
Family Practice Physician

CONTENTS

Foreword

You are holding in your hands one of the MOST NEEDED BOOKS in the 21st Century Christian community!

Living with Faith and Mental Illness is a game-changer for many sincere people who will make the journey through its powerful pages. Author Tara Taylor is a cherished friend and an esteemed staff member from a previous pastorate together. I watched her up close navigate the challenges of faith and mental illness with unbelievable courage, tenacity, and fortitude. The chapters you are about to read give you an authentic and massively helpful roadmap through her own personal challenges.

Many years into her own experience with bipolar disorder, Tara is now a Licensed Professional Counselor. I often remind myself that, "We LEAD people through our STRENGTHS. But we CONNECT to people through our WEAKNESSES." These pages reverberate with both strong wisdom and vulnerable authenticity. She shares in a balanced fashion that gives her readers seasoned, documented wisdom as well as large doses of understanding, compassion, and Biblical hope.

You will also enjoy the chapter written by her outstanding husband, Pastor Terrell Taylor. He, like Tara, stands in a league of his own. He shares powerful insight for anyone who is a family member connected to someone facing mental health challenges. In a Christian world that often delivers cheap "TRT" (Typical Religious Talk), Terrell and Tara cut through the veneer to be an anchor and a true life-source for everyone who reads Living with Faith and Mental Illness.

Years ago, Napoleon Bonaparte said "The greatest leaders of all civilization are those who INSPIRE HOPE." So with that quote in mind, I introduce you to one of the most impactful leaders you have probably met in a long time: Tara Taylor. Drink deep from her wisdom, faith, transparency, and HOPE. And may Tara's journey inspire you with the courage YOU need to face into your own personal future. Just remember: It is never foolish to trust an UNKNOWN FUTURE to a very KNOWN GOD.

Most Sincerely,
Dr. Jeanne Mayo
President & Founder: Youth Leader's Coach
Founder & Director: The Cadre
Youth & Young Adult Director, Victory World Church, Atlanta, Georgia
Executive Director, Atlanta Leadership College
Public speaker, communicator, and author

Section 1

1

Blindsided by Bipolar Disorder

Isaiah 61:3

And to provide for those who grieve in Zion – to bestow on them a crown of beauty instead of ashes, the oil of joy instead of mourning, and a garment of praise instead of a spirit of despair.

Major Depressive Disorder, Bipolar Disorder, Schizoaffective Disorder, Obsessive Compulsive Disorder, Generalized Anxiety Disorder... These are just a few of the mental health diagnoses that, if spoken by a doctor, can trigger feelings of fear, shame, guilt, and humiliation in almost anyone. Often hearing one of these diagnoses can potentially cause one to feel as though your life is completely crumbling all around you. This is just how I felt.

In November of 1998 I began to feel as if I was living in the middle of a scary nightmare of a person I did not even recognize. Up to this point my life had been going along just fine. It was May of 1997, and I had just turned 21 years old. I was graduating Magna Cum Laude from Oral Roberts University and I was honored to be chosen to be the class Graduation Speaker. The very next day, at the ripe age of 21, I very happily said "I Do" to Terrell Taylor, my college sweetheart. I felt like I was the most blessed (good Christians didn't say lucky) girl in the entire world. Life was just beginning for me. Terrell and I were quickly swept into a life as young newlyweds, being in full-time ministry, and discovering that we had a little stowaway with us when we returned from our Hawaiian honeymoon. It was nine months later that we named our little stowaway Trevor. Our oldest son, Trevor, was born exactly nine months after we were married. For those of you who were raised in a small church like I was, you must know that many people could not help but count the months to see if we had kept our sexual purity before marriage. But that is another story for an entirely different book...

On February 4, 1998 our Trevor was born and I was living my dream of being a wife and a mom. Those were the two things I had always wanted more than anything else. My family used to laugh at me when I was a little girl because I would sometimes sit and cry, worrying at the thought that I might one day marry the "wrong" guy. When I wasn't worrying about my impending marriage I was busy sitting on a pillow in our living room trying to get a baby to appear in my tummy, just like some of the ladies at church. I thought – without question – that must definitely be how babies are made because all the pregnant ladies in church would bring pillows to church to sit on. The pillow experiment seemed to work well for them! Little did I know they were just trying to protect their backs and bums from getting sore on those old-fashioned rickety folding chairs. Since marriage and motherhood had always been my number one goal in life everything should have been perfectly pristine. But unfortunately that was not the case.

I look back now and see that mental health issues were quietly brewing just underneath the surface but of course I had no idea what was happening at the time.

I had just graduated with a Bachelor's degree in Organizational and Interpersonal Communications with a minor in Education, had married the love of my life, and was part of a great church. Yet I remember days even during my pregnancy when I would find myself sitting alone on the kitchen floor bawling my eyes out. I felt depressed and so utterly alone. I chalked it up to the fact that I was no longer surrounded by friends 24/7 the way it had been while living life in the college dormitory. Plus, being a newly married couple in ministry – we were living on a modest income and had only one car between us. When my husband was at work I was stuck in a small apartment all day long, very isolated from everyone else. Most of my friends from college had either moved back home after graduation or were simply occupied with their own lives. So a slow, yet steady depression began growing within me, although I did not completely recognize it at the time.

When Trevor was born in February of 1998 I loved being a mom, but there was always a great deal of anxiety surrounding motherhood and life in general for me. I had an anxious personality since I was a young girl and motherhood only magnified it. One of the pastor's wives at the church where my husband was employed had had a baby girl about the same time I had Trevor. We shared many funny mommy stories and would talk about how our days were filled with tiredness, stress, diapers, cleaning, cooking, breastfeeding, and holding the baby all day, trying to get more done than a new mom should ever expect from herself. We both loved being a mom and I looked up to her. She was an amazing pastor's wife, mom, and all-around balanced woman. This was not her first baby and she always seemed more relaxed as a mom than I could ever hope to be. Then one day I unassumingly called the church office to speak to my husband and the administrative assistant who answered the telephone told me the most unexpectedly devastating news – my friend's precious baby girl had died suddenly during the night! This horrifying news, accompanied by an immense fear, shook me to my very core. "How could this happen to her baby? She was a great mom and this wasn't fair! How could God allow her baby to die?" I could not believe it. The fear brought up more questions than answers in me.

When tragedy strikes it challenges everything that we have ever believed. Suddenly all of our neatly crafted beliefs get trampled on and we are left frantically trying to hold on to something that makes sense, something to still be certain of.

If a person has a family history of mental illness or a biological predisposition for it, it is possible that all it takes is simply a trigger, such as a tragedy, to send that person into a full-blown mental health crisis. That is precisely what happened to me. During those next few days the church was helping to plan a funeral for a beautiful baby girl who we all believed went to see Jesus decades too soon. To say I was in distress would most definitely be an understatement. I would find myself in such deep grief that I would sob and be unable to sleep. I could not understand how this could happen and subconsciously asked myself, "What if that had been my child?" Even writing these words carries a certain amount of fear. No parent would dare to imagine what it would be like to bury his or her own child. That is not the way this circle of life is supposed to work. Children are supposed to bury their parents when they are old and gray. It seems quite backward to bury a child whose life had just begun. This is another wretched step in grief in which many people find themselves. It is the confusing and vulnerable step of not having the answers.

While I was going through my inner turmoil and depression I could not at the time see anything except deep darkness and despair, but each time darkness threatened to consume me, my God brought me out with His mighty hand.

So in 1998 when my friend's baby passed away it triggered a genetic predisposition for bipolar disorder. Not only was bipolar disorder beginning to slowly manifest, but because it was undiagnosed and untreated at the time, I actually began to fall into a frightening psychotic episode.

What is bipolar psychosis? "Psychosis is the inability to recognize what is real in the world around you. This is different from what your thoughts and perceptions tell you. People who are experiencing psychosis often have hallucinations or delusions" (Morris, 2016).

When I was growing up I had always believed that if someone was having a psychotic episode then they must most likely be demon possessed. Some Christians were taught this and you may have heard this before. Many of you may think this sounds absurd or antiquated. But nevertheless, I used to believe that someone with a severe mental illness must be possessed by a demon. This false belief is damaging and potentially dangerous to those who are struggling to find freedom and healing from a mental illness. If someone with a mental disorder believes they are possessed by a demon then they are less likely to seek help from a medical professional. I have been a Christian since I was three years old and I am now a Pastor's wife and believe very strongly and deeply in the power of prayer. However, I have learned to also believe in the authority that God has given doctors and the healing that can come through traditional medicine as well. For me, I see clearly how God chose to use psychiatrists and medication to restore me to a place of healing and wholeness.

Unfortunately, when my friend's baby passed away this triggered in me symptoms of bipolar disorder. The disordered thinking began even before the funeral of my friend's baby. I was no longer sleeping and was having difficulty with even day-to-day functioning. This is encumbering enough when you only have to take care of yourself, but add to that having to take care of your nine month old baby! It feels like your world is closing in on you. I remember distinctly a few times when my husband, Terrell, needed to go to work and I would stand at the door and cry, practically begging him to please not leave me alone with the baby. I felt so overwhelmed and was not sure if I could take care of myself, let alone care for our son. At that point neither he, nor I, or anyone else understood what was going on inside me mentally and emotionally. He did his best to lovingly, but firmly, explain that he had to go to work and that I would be just fine. Miraculously through the depression, extreme anxiety, and disordered thinking I still managed to take care of Trevor.

As the funeral was approaching I began attempting to figure out why God would allow this precious baby to die. I started to believe that maybe God had allowed her to die in order to raise her from the dead. Maybe He wanted this to become a national phenomenon to make His name famous throughout America. The more I started to think about this, the more I began to undeniably believe it and there was nothing anyone could have said or done to convince me of anything different. I convinced myself into believing that I would go to the funeral and raise the baby from the dead. All of a sudden I had this surge of energy and my grief became mixed with a manic episode. Mania is the part of bipolar disorder that typically feels good. Most people do not seek medical treatment for mania the way they might for the depressive symptoms of bipolar disorder. The manic phase of bipolar disorder is characterized by an elevated mood, feelings of euphoria, little need for sleep, impulsive and high-risk behavior, and at times, irritability. In severe cases mania can also include delusions and hallucinations like mine did. When people are in a manic phase they may have an extreme amount of energy and confidence but may also become very irritable with those around them. After the funeral, the people who did not agree with me about my desire to raise the baby from the dead found themselves with an earful of my agitation. I thought, "How could they not see it and believe it just like me?" Fortunately, for all who were present at the funeral, I did not end up approaching the casket let alone try to raise the baby from the dead. I imagine that would have been very disturbing and unsettling for the family who was already dealing with an insurmountable amount of grief and confusion. So does this mean that if someone wants to pray for someone to be raised from the dead then they are obviously mentally ill? I would have to answer with an emphatic "No!" The Bible is filled with stories of Jesus and his disciples not only healing the sick but also raising the dead. There are also present day documented accounts of people who have come back to life after having been declared dead. Miracles still exist today, but in my specific situation I realize I was experiencing symptoms of mania and a psychotic break.

During the funeral I had started to feel very weak like I could barely move. My husband ended up carrying me out of the funeral and placing me gently in the car. He drove me to the nearest emergency room because he was concerned and did not know what to do. After waiting in the Emergency Room I saw a kind doctor who called my diagnosis "situational depression". He told me I was obviously grieving and I simply needed some rest and tenderness from family and friends. That evening a friend from church came over and sat with me, fixed me something to eat, and was a listening ear that night and the next day. She showed God's love, not merely with words but just by her very presence. It was refreshing for my soul. Processing my feelings, however, was not enough to put all the chemicals in my brain back into proper balance. After the funeral things in my life continued to be a whirlwind of emotions, irrational thoughts, and strange behavior. Finally, one of the counselors from our church recommended that Terrell take me to a nearby psychiatric hospital to be evaluated. During the evaluation I remember thinking,

"Maybe God will even use this for His glory because I don't believe anything is really mentally wrong with me." For some reason I began to feel the need to prove to God that I would do anything for Him, that I would even die for Him.

I was admitted into a nearby psychiatric hospital, and thankfully it had a Christian division called Rapha, which means, "The Lord my Healer." When you were admitted and requested to be part of the Christian unit of the hospital they presented you with a book entitled, The Search for Significance by Robert McGee. This is one of those books that will completely transform your life if you let it. It deals with the issues that many of us face in life, revealing underlying false beliefs. One of these self-limiting false beliefs addressed by McGee is the belief that says, "I must meet certain standards in order to feel good about myself" (McGee, 1991, p. 40). If we do not conquer this false belief and replace it with the truth of God's Word we will always struggle with our self-concept and self-worth. This false belief that I must meet certain standards in order to feel good about myself is destined to fail miserably. Temporarily we may be able to sustain good behavior and meet these invisible and ever changing standards, but behavior modification which begins on the outside will never be life giving or sustaining. Only God's Word has the transforming power to bring lasting change. This is because the Word of God deals with our inner life, our heart and our thought life. Hebrews 4:12 says, "For the word of God is alive and active. Sharper than any double-edged sword, it penetrates even to dividing soul and spirit, joints and marrow; it judges the thoughts and attitudes of the heart."

Self-limiting beliefs are really nothing more than lies from the enemy and will strangle the very truth of who we are from us if we allow it. I say, "If we allow it" because there is a high calling and responsibility that we each have as children of God. We have within us the capacity to think and the capacity to choose our own belief systems. Based upon our childhood, our circumstances, and our genetic makeup, it may be easier for some to choose to believe the best and to choose to direct their thoughts according to the Word of God. However, whether or not it is easier for you or for me, does not determine where our mindset should go.

Romans 12:2 (AMP) states very clearly:

And do not be conformed to this world [any longer with its superficial values and customs], but be transformed and progressively changed [as you mature spiritually] by the renewing of your mind [focusing on godly values and ethical attitudes], so that you may prove [for yourselves] what the will of God is, that which is good and acceptable and perfect [in His plan and purpose for you].

It has taken me quite a while to realize that there is no shortcut to victory. The Word of God has given us the blueprint for life. God's Word provides us with the roadmap for success in this life and nothing else will suffice. Once we recognize this is a daily battle, we will be more likely to put on the full armor of God found in Ephesians 6 and will no longer be afraid to fight the negative thoughts that may assault us… sometimes even multiple times a day.

Ephesians 6:13-17 says:

Therefore put on the full armor of God, so that when the day of evil comes, you may be able to stand your ground, and after you have done everything, to stand. Stand firm then, with the belt of truth buckled around your waist, with the breastplate of righteousness in place, and with your feet fitted with the readiness that comes from the gospel of peace. In addition to all this, take up the shield of faith, with which you can extinguish all the flaming arrows of the evil one. Take the helmet of salvation and the sword of the Spirit, which is the word of God.

2

Coping with a Mental Diagnosis

2 Corinthians 12:9

But he said to me, "My grace is sufficient for you, for my power is made perfect in weakness." Therefore I will boast all the more gladly about my weaknesses, so that Christ's power may rest on me.

I f you have ever had the unfortunate experience of being admitted into a psychiatric hospital you may understand when I say that at first the very thought of it is mind boggling, at least it was to me. I could not conceive that I, Tara Taylor, honor student, good Christian girl, Chaplain in my dormitory at Oral Roberts University, college graduation speaker, and Music Pastor's wife was sitting in a place in which I did not belong. However, the truth of the matter was I actually did belong there. The structure of the hospital schedule and safety of the environment was exactly what I needed at that time in my life. However, you would have had an extremely difficult time trying to convince me of this fact. I remember one evening getting a call from a family member who kept admonishing me, "Make sure you take your medication." I knew he was only concerned but I was convinced that he was clearly mistaken. At that time I did not believe I needed medication and replied that I did not even think the medication was real. "They're probably just giving me a sugar pill!" I exclaimed. At the time I believed what I was saying, but looking back I am glad they were not just giving me a sugar pill. I do not know the name of that very first medication, but my guess is that it was an anti-psychotic. Once I realized they were giving me more than a sugar pill I began to feel afraid to take the medication. I was terrified it would alter my brain too much and cause horrendous side-effects. The ironic part is I needed it to alter my brain enough to cause everything to come into correct alignment. Furthermore, the side-effects I was already experiencing were worse than any the medication was most likely going to cause.

I clearly remember the fear and apprehension I had of taking medication, yet it still astonishes me each time I meet someone who is having extreme mental health issues and yet states, "I'm afraid of the side-effects." With as much compassion as I can possibly muster I feel compelled to remind them of the side-effects of the depression, anxiety, or whatever brand of mental illness that is plaguing them. I may say something such as, "Please remember that not wanting to get out of bed for days, wanting to end your life, and isolating yourself from loved ones are already detrimental side-effects that are occurring from not taking medication." Sometimes that helps people to change their perspective, but sometimes it does not. If you are reading this today and you suffer with a mental illness, please recognize that you are most likely already suffering side-effects from the mental illness. I do not want to minimize the fear of side-effects because I know fear from taking prescription medication is real, but never forget that you have a voice and are always entitled to speak up about your medical care and your concerns. You are the best advocate you will ever have and you are the most qualified person to work alongside your doctor to discover the right combination of medications that can help you move on with your life and be successful at being the best you can be. It does sometimes take trial and error to get the medication just right. At first I do believe I was overly medicated but I spoke up as best I could and the doctor made adjustments to the medication. Your brain chemistry also changes over time and the medication that once worked for you may stop working after a while. This is when you have to be willing to be courageous and try a new medication if needed. The most important thing to remember is as long as you have breath in your body, you have hope.

During my first stay in the Psychiatric Hospital for the first few days, I truly believed God wanted me to die and then wanted to raise me from the dead to prove how powerful He was. This erroneous belief stemmed from me not seeing my friend's baby come back to life and not being able to believe that God wouldn't have wanted that to happen. I had this warped mindset that God needed me to help Him be known around the nation as the God of miracles. This was faulty theology. Yes, we are to be obedient to Him but when our estimation of ourselves and what God *needs* us to do becomes inflated we subconsciously dismiss the Sovereignty of God. As much as I wish it were not true, bad things do indeed happen to very good people. As painful as it is, it is painfully true. I do not have the answers as to why my friend's baby died. One thing I know is this - in the end God will right every wrong. My friend will one day be reunited with her precious daughter. One day there will be no more pain, no more death, no more crying, and no more suffering. Revelation 21:4 says, "He will wipe every tear from their eyes. There will be no more death or mourning or crying or pain, for the old order of things has passed away."

We must always remember this life is not the end of the

story. If we forget this important truth and believe this life is all there is then we will be without a doubt "people most to be pitied" (1 Corinthians 15:1).

As days progressed I continued to hold on to my delusional belief that God had chosen me to die and come back to life in order to display His power. I remember one day in particular when Terrell looked at me and calmly said, "Tara, if this does not happen to you by today at 4:00 pm can we agree that you were wrong?" I remember reluctantly assenting to this idea but when the agreed upon time came and went it was still almost impossible for me to let go of this delusion. I felt I would be giving up on God or even worse, that I might be disappointing Him. I wanted Him to know I was willing to even die for Him. This idea may sound noble and maybe in some ways it is, but also in many ways I was placing too great a responsibility on myself and what I must do for God. Knowing you have a specific destiny is essential for a life to be lived with purpose. However, my truth was convoluted in such a way that it was heavily mixed with a major dose of psychosis and faulty beliefs.

Part of what made my psychotic episode so confusing is that it was strongly intertwined with a spiritual belief system. Some of the things I was holding onto were Biblically based, like believing that God could raise the dead. However, they were delusional because they were not things God was showing me, but I believed they were.

The book, <u>Blue Genes</u>, by Paul Meier states, "We have worked with literally hundreds of psychotic individuals over the past thirty years, and our experience is that Christians have 'Christian delusions,' Muslims have 'Muslim delusions,' Buddhists have 'Buddhist delusions,' and atheists have secular or more political delusions. Christians who become psychotic often become delusionally grandiose, thinking that they possess supernatural revelations or abilities" (Meier, 2005, p. 75).

My psychotic episode was quite mixed with me wanting desperately to see a miracle. I do not believe anything is innately wrong with wanting to witness a miracle, but when you want it more than you want to simply know Christ then it can quickly take you down the wrong path.

There were times in the hospital when it was obvious the staff was becoming increasingly frustrated with me. They needed me to be the patient and not attempt to be a minister and yet that was extremely difficult for me. Almost immediately after being admitted into the hospital I met a young lady who had recently been diagnosed with schizophrenia. Her parents were devastated and just wanted their daughter to get better. I decided maybe this was my assignment as well and proceeded to pray for her. I do not know if she ever got better or not, but I remember one of the nurses there admonishing me to focus on myself. However, because initially I did not believe I had a problem, that was challenging for me to do. By the time it was all said and done I had been in this psychiatric hospital a total of three different times within a three month period. I was admitted in November of 1998, December of 1998, and then for the final time in January of 1999. It took a while before I got the accurate diagnosis of bipolar disorder. It was scary being in the hospital at times and not knowing exactly what was wrong with me. As the doctors and counselors were trying to figure out my diagnosis they would ask me many questions such as, "Tara, do you hear voices?" That was a question I remember far too well. Somehow in the midst of not being completely in my right mind I still understood that the answers to these questions were extremely important. "Do I hear voices?" I asked. "Do you mean thoughts in my head?" I wanted to be sure I answered these questions correctly to receive the right diagnosis. Even while being in a delusional state, there is still a sense of human dignity that we possess.

If you are reading this as a Mental Health Professional please remember that everyone has an innate sense of human dignity. Always strive to preserve that in your clients. Everyone, whether, they have a mental illness or not needs to feel that they are a part of the solution. They need to be included in their treatment plan and spoken to with the utmost of care and respect. Seemingly simple things such as your tone of voice with a patient can be the difference in them believing they are worthy of love and respect versus them giving up on themselves. People need to know they have purpose and destiny and a mental health crisis does not have to be the end of their story. However, many times they look to you as the Mental Health Professional to believe in them and to see them through eyes of faith and love. Have the courage to look past their diagnosis and see the individual becoming strong with the ability to overcome any obstacle. Be their advocate as you walk along their side!

While undergoing psychiatric treatment it was embarrassing at times when I would stop to ponder, "What do these people think about me?" Some of my behavior was incredibly bizarre and one of the counselors at the hospital had actually been in seminary with my husband just a year and a half before this time. I knew Terrell had to deal with his own form of embarrassment. I felt badly for him but knew I had to focus on myself and find my own emotional and mental stability. Unfortunately, he would have to fend for himself emotionally and mentally. Terrell was wise and continued to reach out to friends who were influential in our lives.

One couple who were amazing friends and stepped in when it would have been more convenient to step out were Pastors Reggie and Candi Stewart. Reggie and Candi had been friends since college and knew us even while we were dating. Candi also happened to be employed as a counselor at the psychiatric hospital where I was now a resident. I remember times when she would come to my hospital room just to see me and check on me. Seeing her familiar and caring face was emotionally stabilizing. She never treated me like I was a mental patient. She would simply check on me and love on me. Pastors Reggie and Candi even went so far as to let Terrell and Trevor stay with them for a few days while I was in the hospital. They knew he needed a safe place to land and it probably was not a good idea for him to spend too much time home alone with his own thoughts. He needed to know that everything was going to be okay. I do not know what Reggie and Candi believed during that time or if they truly knew that our marriage and ministry were going to be restored, but their acts of selfless love were invaluable for Terrell and me.

During that time Terrell also reached out to a professional counselor who helped him focus on his own need for inner healing. He went to his sessions wanting to talk about me and the mess that bipolar disorder had made of his marriage and ministry, but she wisely refocused him and said, "Terrell, let's talk about you." I am thankful for these people who God put in our path at just the right time and season of our lives.

When you are going through a difficult time, who you choose to surround yourself with will either make life more sustainable or can make your situation feel even more devastating. The people that were in our lives ended up being lifelines for Terrell and me and I will forever be grateful for them.

3

Terrell's Journey

2 Corinthians 1:3-4
Praise be to the God and Father or our Lord Jesus Christ,
the Father of compassion and the God of all comfort, who
comforts us in all our troubles, so that we can comfort those
in any trouble with the comfort we ourselves have received
from God.

The next words you read are written from my husband, Terrell's perspective. As we know, mental illness does not only affect the person diagnosed but it also touches the lives of the family and close friends. Here is Terrell's journey written from a place of authenticity and transparency.

The title, Living with Faith and Mental Illness, may seem like a contradiction, but in reality it is all too often simply ignored. Not only does the individual with the illness suffer, but those close to the person suffer as well. I am such a person.

God did not create us to be alone, and it so happened that God ordained for me to be the covenant partner of

Tara. When we married on May 4th, 1997 in Tulsa, Oklahoma (better known as the faith capital of the United States), we wrote our own vows. The words "for better or for worse" were taken out because we felt like that phrase did n't belong in our vows. After all, we reasoned, they were not words of faith. But little did we know that 18 months later we would be facing a "for better or for worse" situation.

Hebrews 11:1 (NKJV) says, "Now faith is the substance of things hoped for, the evidence of things not seen." This scripture is one of the most often quoted but least understood. Christians in the faith movement often ignore the fact that faith has to have an object. For Believers that object is the person of Jesus Christ, not faith itself. Faith in our faith will not suffice in times of personal tragedy and difficulty. The substance of what we hope for has to be rooted in the Author and Finisher of our faith (Hebrews 12:2). When we fix our eyes on Jesus, He becomes the focus in the midst of our storm.

And there was a storm brewing in my young marriage. When I had dated Tara, I met and heard stories of some of her family members who had some kind of mental illness. Many of them were geniuses and well-educated. But I did not take into account that Tara could possibly have the same or similar diagnosis. After all, I was in love, and we all know that love is blind. Truthfully, only God knew the storm that was about to hit my young family. I remember having a conversation with my friend's wife just weeks prior to Tara's psychotic episode. She told me that my son Trevor, who was only nine months at the time, would be an anchor in my marriage. Honestly, I had no idea what she was talking about. An anchor in my marriage was not needed as far as I knew. We were doing great. We had a new job, a new baby, and a new house all within a year of our new marriage. Life was good. But there was a storm brewing and God knew that an anchor was needed.

I thank God for Trevor, who is now 19 years old, for being in my life at the time of our family storm. He was an unplanned honeymoon baby, but planned by God. He was my mainstay as I struggled to figure out what was happening to Tara. I was blindsided by the blow of mental illness as it tried to tear my family apart. But I had to take care of my son, not realizing that my son was taking care of me. I remember calling two of my friends and asking them to come over and pray with me. I was broken, angry, and confused. I had taken our wedding album and started to cut up those beautiful pictures of my bride and me. I thought it was possibly over, but my friends stopped me from completing my task and said, "Don't do it. You might regret that one day." As I prayed and wrestled with God concerning my family's future He gave me the strength to persevere. A lady from my mother's church, who had no idea what was going on, called my mom and told her to tell me that my wife was going to be okay. She specifically had a word from the Lord and I believed it. It did not make my circumstance any easier, but it gave me the faith and confidence I needed to persevere. Hebrews 10:35-36 says, "So do not throw away your confidence; it will be richly rewarded. You need to persevere so that when you have done the will of God, you will receive what he has promised."

Now I am on the other side of the promise. Tara and I have three wonderful boys and 20 years of covenant marriage. We pastor a life-giving church and have incredible family and friends who love and support us. Over the years we have had our ups and downs, but have learned to live with faith and mental illness. Tara has done an incredible job of helping me understand her

diagnosis and her needs. I have educated myself and have done my best to be a help to Tara, while not allowing this illness to define her. She will tell you that I routinely forget that she has been diagnosed with bipolar disorder. I admit that part of me only wants to see the faith and not the mental illness. If you are reading this book and have a loved one who is struggling with the same or similar illness, be encouraged because God is with you. He has chosen you to be the father, mother, sister, brother, husband, wife, son, or daughter of someone who needs your love and support. Life is a unique journey for all of us. And living with faith and mental illness is a part of your unique journey. So embrace it. Find strength in it. And know that God has not forgotten you.

4

My Path to Healing

I Peter 5:10
And the God of all grace, who called you to his eternal glory in Christ, after you have suffered a little while, will himself restore you and make you strong, firm and steadfast.

The psychiatric hospital did offer many moments of healing for me. These moments came through reading books like <u>The Search for Significance</u> by McGee, attending group and individual therapy sessions, and through educating myself about bipolar disorder. These moments also came in the form of people who I always secretly hoped were angels in disguise. One young woman I met had come in one day to visit her friend, but when she met me she lovingly included me in the conversation and assured me I was doing something positive by being in the hospital and getting the help and support I needed. She reminded me to be proud of myself for taking care of me and getting medical help. She also gave me her phone number to call if I needed anything and even later came back to visit and brought me chocolate, colored pencils, and coloring books to help me relax and pass the time. These gestures may seem small to some, but they were really grand gestures of love. I was simply a stranger to her - someone she had just met in a mental health facility who would most likely never be able to return the favor, yet she went out of her way to display kindness to me. I will never forget her and the lesson she taught me. It is commendable to perform acts of kindness for friends and family and we all should. However, how often do we perform acts of kindness for strangers who may never be able to repay us? I pray that even today she is blessed beyond measure because she sowed seeds of kindness into a person who was confused and hurting. She displayed the love of God in a tangible and genuine way without expecting anything in return.

Since I was in this psychiatric hospital three times within a three month period, one of those times happened to fall right around Christmas time. It had been my second time there at this point. I was still so manic that I was in a major psychotic episode. Life was difficult and everything seemed so unclear. I felt that people were out to harm me. I also falsely believed there were secret messages attached to almost everything. The brain is a fascinating organ and has the incredible ability to play tricks on us when we least suspect. Had I more quickly listened to my family and friends and believed them that things I was hearing and believing were not true, it could have definitely shortened my time in and out of the hospital, but I was convinced I knew better than everyone else. That is part of the frightening aspect of psychosis… very few people are willing to renounce their outlandish ideas and thoughts. During a psychotic episode thoughts seem so real and valid.

If you have ever seen the movie a "Beautiful Mind" you will understand what I am trying to explain. The beginning of the movie is as real to those of us who are watching as it was to mathematical genius, John Nash, who was diagnosed with schizophrenia. Unless you have personally experienced psychosis, it is puzzling to understand and sometimes difficult to feel compassion for someone suffering with psychosis. It is perplexing to understand how they could believe things that are so bizarre to those whose minds are functioning normally. Because I have had the unfortunate privilege of experiencing psychosis first hand I refrain from calling people "crazy" or laughing at those individuals who may be walking up and down the street talking to themselves. When you have walked a day or two in someone else's shoes it completely transforms your perspective. If you allow God to deal with your heart, He will take those places that used to judge others and replace it with a soft heart that is filled with compassion for those who are hurting.

When tragedy strikes, we all have a choice. We can either choose resentment and bitterness and ask, "Why me?" or we can choose to push through the pain and the unanswered questions and say, "God must have a plan." Believing that God has a plan when you believe you received the raw end of the deal takes faith, patience, and hope. I wish I could say I always had that hope, but the truth is I started this journey feeling very self-righteous. I would think about my own goodness… how I remained pure until marriage, didn't cuss, smoke, or drink. I had always obeyed my parents growing up, and never showed any serious signs of rebellion. So at the age of 23, being newly married to a Music Pastor, having a nine month old baby boy, and being diagnosed with bipolar disorder did not fit into my neatly crafted box. Inside my theological box were beliefs such as, "If you serve God with all your heart then bad things won't happen to you." Another false belief I had erected in my mind was, "Bad things happen to those people who have sin in their lives." Looking back I see these were symptoms of a much deeper problem… these were indicators that I was dealing with faulty theology and toxic faith. During this time of hurt and confusion a counselor referred me to a book entitled, Toxic Faith, written by Stephen Arterburn and Jack Felton. Arterburn sums up the hope his book offered to many people when it was first released. He states, "We had cut in on the dance of self-deception and introduced tired dancers to a God who could not be manipulated and whose love could not be earned" (Arterburn & Felton, 2001, pg. xii).

I believe that despite the tremendous heartache we

may feel at times, when it comes to our faith, we who are Believers are actually relieved when we find out our God is Sovereign. I am glad to know that my God, Creator of this great universe cannot be manipulated by anything, including my perceived goodness or self-righteousness. When we stop and think about it, it is my pride that says, "God you must do what I am asking you to do and I do not care if your plan is different." For the first eight years after my experience with psychosis I could not comprehend why my Heavenly Father would allow me to experience such pain when I did not feel like I deserved it. However, something clicked after eight years and I reached a miraculous place where I was able to look up to heaven and say, "Thank you Lord that I experienced that season of mental suffering and turmoil." I had come to a point where I knew there was purpose attached to my pain. That was also when the Holy Spirit clearly spoke to my heart to go back to school and pursue my Master's Degree in Professional Counseling.

I wonder if I felt a little the way Joseph in the Old Testament must have felt. After being thrown into a pit and being falsely imprisoned Joseph came to a place in Genesis 50:20 (NASB) where he could boldly say, "As for you, you meant evil against me, but God meant it for good in order to bring about this present result, to preserve many people alive." We must not be unaware of Satan's devices. He intends evil against us, but God in His Sovereignty takes the brokenness with which

Satan meant to destroy us and transforms it into a beautiful and living masterpiece. And that masterpiece is not just for our benefit, but also for the benefit of others. God will take our place of pain and turn it into a place of purpose and healing for others.

Being in a psychiatric facility around Christmas time was difficult, especially since that was Trevor's first Christmas. I felt so conflicted about being in the hospital near Christmas. Part of me knew I needed to be there where it was safe and I could get stabilized on my medication. But the other part of me, felt so guilty for being in a mental hospital at Christmas time while my baby was home without his mother. Trevor had just learned to walk and I had already missed that. He was an early walker and everyone marveled that he was walking at only nine months old. When I was told that Trevor had started walking I did not even have the emotional strength to focus on the fact that I was missing some of my baby's 1st milestones.

A couple days before Christmas I ended up asking the psychiatrist if I could be released from the hospital since it was my baby's first Christmas. He reluctantly agreed. The strange part is I secretly wanted him to say "no". I knew that as long as I had asked to be released I could relinquish the guilt because truthfully I was scared to go home and knew I was not mentally ready, but he released me to go home despite his reservations. Due to the fact that I went home before I was ready it would be only a matter of weeks before I would find myself back in the psychiatric hospital once again.

Some people have to deal with certain side-effects when adjusting to a new medication and psychiatric medication is not exempt from side-effects. I found myself having gained 40 pounds in about 40 days. Some of this was due to the medication and some was due to the fact that I was eating non-stop, especially sweets, which had always been my weakness. Food was offered in plentiful portions and I did not see the need to exercise self-control since I felt I was already in such an unfair place. I have come to realize that no one except for me ever attends my pity-parties. At the time the parties were filled with shame, stigma, and don't forget self-indulgence of sweets. It seems many of us when we feel we have been unfairly treated by God will turn to something to feel better. This is the reason many people will self-medicate. I noticed while a patient in the hospital that I was the only person I knew that did not also have a substance abuse issue or at least smoked cigarettes. At one point all my friends were going outside to smoke and I told the nurse maybe I would try it. In her wisdom she said, "Let's not start that while you're in here." It is amusing to realize that even as adults sometimes we just want to fit in with those we are surrounded by. This is one reason why if you are going through a vulnerable season it is best to not surround yourself with people that are going to have a negative effect on you. Surround yourself with people who are strong and are able to remind you how resilient you are and that you can conquer whatever situation you are going through.

Not only did the hospital have their regular psychiatric ward for those dealing with mental illness, but they also had a unit for those struggling to overcome eating disorders. There were times we would all go to the cafeteria together for meal time. I enjoyed making friends while in the hospital, including those from the eating disorder unit. I would overhear some of the patients from my unit whisper that they wished they *only* had an eating disorder. I guess it is simply true what they say, "The grass always looks greener on the other side of the fence." My mania was mixed with undeniable confidence and with a lack of a filter on my words. I confidently told the patients with eating disorders one day, "Don't you see that Satan wants to kill you and you're helping him?" My approach probably could have used some tact but they did not seem offended in the least and we dialogued about their issues and about mine. There was something inside me even then that was passionate to see people break free from their bondages. Because I did not have an eating disorder, it seemed quite simple for me to tell them to just start eating again, but for them it was a daily battle they had to fight and that had the potential to take their lives.

If you are in a battle, keep fighting! Do not ever give up and do not dare surrender to whatever is trying to conquer you! The key to fighting a war and not giving up must begin and end with the Word of God. I John 4:4 (NASB) says, "You are from God, little children, and have overcome them; because greater is He who is in you than he who is in the world." The Word of God and the power of the Holy Spirit is what we need to be permanently delivered and set free from negative mindsets and false belief systems. That is why the Word of God is called the Sword of the Spirit. Hebrews 4:12 says, "For the word of God is alive and active. Sharper than any double-edged sword, it penetrates even to dividing soul and spirit, joints and marrow; it judges the thoughts and attitudes of the heart."

Being set free from damaging mind sets and thought patterns that seek to destroy our life is a battle we will fight while in this body. Until Jesus comes and establishes His reign on the earth we must daily put on our armor to fortify ourselves against the enemy. Everyone has different things with which they must contend. It is imperative that we do not look around at how our problems seem so much worse than our friend's problems, but that we remember the same God who can set one person free can also set us free. We never know when our breakthrough and freedom will suddenly happen!

2 Corinthians 10:3-5 says:

Though we live in the world, we do not wage war as the world does. The weapons we fight with are not the weapons of the world. On the contrary, they have divine power to demolish strongholds. We demolish arguments and every pretension that sets itself up against the knowledge of God, and we take captive every thought to make it obedient to Christ.

Sometimes people mistakenly think that being a Christian means being a nice and passive person. No, on the contrary we are called to be warriors. Warriors must fight or they will get slaughtered. If you are getting slaughtered by the voices of the enemy or life situations maybe it is time to begin to see yourself as the warrior that you are. You may not feel like a warrior but that is irrelevant. According to Ephesians 6:10 you are strong in the Lord and in His power. Whether you believe it or not does not change the truth of God's Word, and if you struggle to believe it I challenge you to begin to declare it anyway.

Rick Joyner wrote a powerful book entitled, <u>The Final Quest</u>, which depicts a vision He was given by the Lord. Joyner (1996, p. 26) writes the following:

As I looked more closely at the army of the Lord, the situation seemed even more discouraging. Only a small number were fully dressed in their armor. Many only had one or two pieces of their armor on; some did not have any at all. A large number were already wounded. Most of those who had all their armor still had very small shields, which I knew would not protect them from the onslaught that was coming. Very few of those who were fully armed were adequately trained to use their weapons.

We must not only be aware of Satan's schemes but also be prepared to use our spiritual weapons when he comes against us. For example, if he begins to tell you that you are not worthy of God's love and acceptance you must open your mouth and begin to declare that you have on the "breastplate of righteousness" (Eph. 6:14) and that you are righteous not because of what you have done but because of what Jesus did on the cross (2 Cor. 5:21). Speak the Word of God out loud on a consistent basis because Romans 10:17 declares, "Consequently, faith comes from hearing the message, and the message is heard through the word of Christ." It might not be instantaneous, but consistently speaking the Word of God will begin to transform your thoughts from what you used to think of yourself to what God thinks about you.

When I was finally released from the hospital for the last time in January 1999 I felt like I was damaged goods. It is extremely difficult to be a Christian whose husband is in full-time ministry where everyone in town knows you and to have been in a psychiatric hospital three times in a matter of three months. One of Satan's weapons is to throw a blanket of self-defeating shame over us. That blanket of secret, self-defeating shame felt like a weighted blanket threatening to consume me. Shame is toxic. It makes you feel like a second-class citizen unworthy of what other people are worthy of.

When I was released from the hospital I told Terrell to let me run into the grocery store to pick up a few items. Going to the grocery store surely sounds like a simple errand, but when I walked into that store all of a sudden I felt like I had a flashing neon sign on my forehead declaring, "Just released from a mental institution." I felt like I had a scarlet letter on my chest and that everyone could see it. "Tara, be rational" I told myself. "No one in here even knows you just got out of a mental hospital" but that rationale could not take away the feeling of stigma and shame.

One of the greatest treasures of healing for me came through people who treated me normally despite knowing what I had been through. Many times we are hurt by people, but if we allow it we can also experience love and healing through people as well. This will never happen if we shrink back. During this time in my life of being in and out of the hospital I had been inconsistent on my job and was terrified to call and ask for my job back. After a little bit of time I got a job through a temporary agency. It was an 8 to 5 office job, but it is amazing how that job started increasing my self-esteem. I started feeling like I had a sense of purpose once again. Then about two years later when my temporary position had ended, I mustered up the courage to call and ask for my previous job back. My previous supervisor graciously accepted me and rehired me. Sometimes it merely takes five seconds of courage to do the next brave thing. Before I made the phone call I experienced tremendous anxiety when I would even think of calling, letting her know what I had been through, and asking if she would consider giving me another chance at working there. She was wise and initially hired me on a part-time basis, allowed me to prove myself once again, and then I became her next full-time hire. God's grace shone brightly through everyday people, who through love unknowingly delivered an extra layer of healing to my soul. My soul, which had been so broken, was beginning to mend again. I was starting to feel whole and validated little by little.

5

Damaging Words

Ephesians 4:32
Be kind and compassionate to one another, forgiving each
other, just as in Christ God forgave you.

Through many years of sitting in multiple church services and also being closely involved in ministry I have seen first-hand the potential that words spoken from a platform and by a person in authority can have on the listeners. There were times I would be at a special church event or conference and the issue of mental illness or depression would be mentioned and something insensitive would be said. I remember attending a powerful women's conference with famous speakers in attendance. One well-meaning speaker was talking about the work she does with young ladies who are struggling with self-worth, unplanned pregnancy, mental health issues, etc. and she made the comment, "You can't medicate a demon." Ouch! This simple comment not only made me feel condemned for taking medication for bipolar disorder but I began to wonder, "Was I demon-possessed?" At this point in my journey I was pretty certain that I was not demon-possessed but the comment almost derailed me. Looking back, I do not believe she meant any harm by the comment. Hopefully she was not against psychiatric medication. She most likely meant that some of the young ladies in her program needed more than just medication, but I was not hearing her through regular filtering methods. My ears heard her words through stigma, shame, and brokenness.

We often speak about those who see the world through rose-colored glasses or the opposite spectrum - those who see things through broken or stained glasses. At that time in my life I was not only seeing the world through broken glasses but I was also hearing the world through the filter of embarrassment and shame. I was ashamed of having been a resident in a psychiatric hospital and I did not want anyone else to find out what I had been through. I had done things during those three months in and out of the hospital that were embarrassing and completely out of character. When people are in a severe manic state or dealing with psychosis they will most likely behave in ways that are outside of their normal character and personality. However, when the medication begins to do its job and their brain chemicals start to balance out, they normally feel a sense of humiliation when they realize some of the things they did or said while in a manic phase or while in psychosis.

Unfortunately, in the time it takes to acclimate to the right medication you may find yourself without some friends that you had before the manic or psychotic episode. This is unfortunate but clearly understandable. I was a lot to handle during those times and there were some people that chose to back away. When I began to realize that, although it was hurtful, I am aware that people had to protect themselves emotionally. As a Licensed Professional Counselor I often talk to clients about setting proper boundaries and so the logical side of me is completely aware that people have to set boundaries. I said some things to people that were hurtful and acted in ways that were bizarre so it only makes sense that some would choose to distance themselves. In life we have the ability to choose what we focus on. Each day presents a new opportunity. Will I choose to focus on those who have rejected me or will I focus on those who love me and want to spend time with me? There will always be a choice. The beauty comes in realizing that only I can make that choice. It is sometimes a daily decision. The fear of rejection is real and affects us whether we are the patient like I was in 1998, or the professional counselor that I am today. Rejection is rejection. The person who is free from the root of rejection and can look it in the eye and shake it off is the person who has learned to gain control over his or her emotions. These are the people who know they were made to be victorious in this life. When we understand the depths of His love for us, we will understand that nothing we have done will ever be able to separate us from His love. I was not myself during those three months of mental confusion but of course initially no one knew quite what was wrong with me. They only knew that some of my behavior was bizarre. However, there were also many people who reached out and loved me in spite of myself. That is when you feel surrounded by the unconditional love of God shining brightly through His people.

Romans 8:35 states:

Who shall separate us from the love of Christ? Shall trouble or hardship or persecution or famine or nakedness or danger or sword? As it is written: "For your sake we face death all day long; we are considered as sheep to be slaughtered." No, in all these things we are more than conquerors through him who loved us. For I am convinced that neither death nor life, neither angels nor demons, neither the present or the future, nor any powers, neither height nor depth, nor anything else in all creation, will be able to separate us from the love of God that is in Christ Jesus our Lord.

6

The Genetic Component of Mental Illness

Psalm 25:20

Guard my life and rescue me; let me not be put to shame, for I take refuge in you.

Maybe there is a part of me that wishes I could say that I have no idea how I came to have a mental disorder or that I am a unique case in my family, but that is not the case. Many times mental illness has a strong genetic component and tends to run in families. There have been several people in my family who have struggled with mental illness. Some of them have been able to get stabilized on their medication and get their illness under control. For others the illness wreaked havoc on their life and the lives of their loved ones and eventually destroyed their destiny. I have some loved ones who because of the torment of their mental disorder eventually took their own life. The emotional pain was too intense and the mental confusion too derailing.

If you have not suffered with depression, bipolar

disorder, schizophrenia or another mental illness it may be extremely difficult to comprehend how life can get to a point where death seems like a beautiful escape. The heartbreaking reality is that suicide is ALWAYS a permanent solution to a temporary problem.

On my darkest days, there were times I wanted to die and almost dared to pray to die. Fortunately for my destiny's sake and the sake of my family, I was afraid to kill myself, but I secretly wished something would happen to me so I could die. "Then my misery would end," I thought.

Suicidal ideation always focuses inward and falsely tells itself that others would be happier if they were no longer here. At the time I was not thinking about my family at all. Life seemed miserable and purposeless. I did not see any hope. Apart from the depression that I would feel at times, the anxiety also tried to swallow my soul and doing even minor chores felt like trying to lift a six-ton elephant over my head. Depression, whether bipolar depression or unipolar depression will try and overtake you if left untreated.

While I was growing up my mother was diagnosed with Major Depressive Disorder. Written below are the thoughts and words of my mom, Hattie Wadlington, as she describes her painful yet personal experience with depression.

I had the unrelenting feeling of loss and grief, the passing from day to night, slowly ticking away minute by minute, unbelievable monotony and boredom, all of these negative feelings were magnified. This is only a surface explanation of what it felt like to be in the dark claws of clinical depression. I felt too ashamed to go beyond the safety of my house for fear of seeing someone who knew me. If that were to occur, how would I explain the deep darkness that I felt so obviously surrounded me and that was so unexplainable? I was in such a pit of despair. I had abruptly stopped working, stopped attending church, and would hardly leave my house to even go to the grocery store. I felt like a failure. My precious pastor's wife, Marie Daniel, would call and leave messages on my answering machine because I had long since stopped answering the telephone. She would say, "This is not the end of the story. Do you hear me Hattie?" I thought that was so kind of her, but felt she was going to be in for a huge disappointment because I fully believed this was not going to have a happy ending and I would be a great disappointment for her. In fact, though I never would have admitted it to a psychiatrist, there were invasive fleeting thoughts from time to time of how I could bring my misery to a swift ending. I felt so overwhelmed by life, sometimes I would stand and stare out of my kitchen window in the morning and watch people driving to work, taking their children to school, moving back and forth with some designated purpose of which I had none. Strangely enough, if you would have told me 24 hours before it occurred that this horribly insane nightmare would soon be over, I would not have believed you. As I look back now, it has been almost 15 years since my abundant life of being able to give and receive love was restored to me. At the time, I could not muster up any belief in myself, but thank God there was enough stored away in my spirit that responded to His Word as I read it in the wee hours one morning, "Commit your works to the Lord, and your thoughts will be established" (Proverbs 16:3, NKJV). That morning something stirred in my spirit that I had not experienced in a very long time. I experienced a confirmation deep within me, affirming that He would make the crooked places in my life straight. His Word confirmed that which seemed hard for me, He would make easy. Somehow He did just what He promised. It has now been almost 15 years of freedom from that dark place of bondage and despair. Never give up because God won't give up on you. Even if you feel you don't believe in Him, He still believes in you!

7

Healing Words

Proverbs 16:24

Gracious words are a honeycomb, sweet to the soul and healing to the bones.

I am so thankful for my mom being restored back to soundness of mind. Her deliverance and healing were different from mine. Hers was more instantaneous but my life's journey through bipolar disorder has not been as supernatural. God had a journey for me that included me having to have the courage to try different medications and to persevere even at times when it felt it was not working. Have enough humility to seek medical help. Years after being released from the hospital I thought that I must have been completely healed from bipolar disorder because there was a period of time where I did not have to take medication for a few years and did not have any manic or depressive symptoms. However, there came a time when I found myself not wanting to get out of bed in the mornings and just wanting to take naps all day if I could, sometimes up to three naps a day. It was during this time that God used my former pastor's wife, Jeanne Mayo, to minister life and hope to me. She must have sensed that something was not quite right because one day after church she asked me how I was doing. "I'm fine," I politely answered. She pried further, "No, how are you really doing?" she asked. "Well" I said, "I pray and I read my Bible but I don't ever want to get out of bed and I have to force myself to do even the smallest things." She looked at me lovingly, but intently and said, "Sometimes not going to see a doctor is not faith at all, but it is pride." Those words spoken at the right time, were what Proverbs 25:11 (NASB) refers to as, "Like apples of gold in settings of silver is a word spoken in right circumstances." I needed that timely word from Jeanne. I could have chosen to get offended or let myself stay rooted in pride, but when you know someone is speaking the truth to you in love you are wise to listen. God used that word to set me free from the shame of seeking medical help. I knew God was speaking through Jeanne and using her to be His mouthpiece. I made the decision to humble myself and I called the doctor the next day.

I shudder to think how long that bout of depression could have lasted had I stubbornly refused to take action. In our journey of healing we have to be determined to be our own advocate. No one can do it for you. Maybe they can make the appointment for you, but after a while your love for yourself needs to be greater than your apathy of remaining the same. I know as well as anyone how painful it is to suffer with bipolar depression. I will admit that was not my last time experiencing depression, but it was the last time that I was confused about whether or not I should contact my doctor.

Some people will ask me if they need to go see a psychiatrist for medications for mental illness or if they can simply go to their primary care physician. The answer to that will depend on a few variables. If you are suffering from mild depression then a primary care doctor many times will feel comfortable writing you a prescription for an anti-depressant. However, if you are suffering with severe depression, bipolar disorder, schizophrenia, or anything more severe than mild depression I would highly recommend making an appointment with a psychiatrist. Psychiatrists are specialists in the field of mental health. If you had cancer you would see an oncologist, if you had severe arthritis you would see a rheumatologist, and similarly if you have a mental illness I recommend seeing a doctor who specializes in mental illnesses which is a psychiatrist.

8

Contagious Courage

Joshua 1:9
Have I not commanded you? Be strong and courageous. Do
not be terrified; do not be discouraged, for the Lord your God
will be with you wherever you go.

The way God connected me with the friends He knew I would need still amazes me. I have come to realize that courage can be contagious. When people share their story of triumph over a painful past it gives others a tremendous confidence boost and the needed courage to also lay aside the mask of pretending. It seems more people are becoming weary of the mask of pretense and the blanket of shame that Satan wants to use to weigh us down. God sent me a friend during college named Ronda. Ronda is one of those one in a million types of friends and we instantly bonded. She shared with me her trials and triumphs and also that she had been diagnosed with bipolar disorder a few years earlier. I did not know at the time that I would have the opportunity to understand this diagnosis first-hand. It was one and a half years after graduation when I received the same diagnosis as Ronda. She was in my life as a breath of fresh air and a source of consistent encouragement. Ronda taught me that it is okay to laugh at myself and to not take everything so seriously. If you were ever the *good girl* or *good guy* who felt you did not deserve bad things to happen and all of a sudden mental illness strikes, it shakes the core of your image of yourself. You are no longer the same person who was always able to hold it all together and who fit into some perceived image of perfection. Now you are fully aware that you too are a sinner who has been saved by grace. Whether you struggle with a particular sin or have been diagnosed with a particular sickness, we are all in need of the transforming grace of our Savior.

The diagnosis of bipolar disorder shook my image of a perfectionistic Tara who had it all together. I could no longer hold together my unblemished image, because now, suddenly it was unquestionably blemished. Although sickness and sin are two different results from the fall of Adam in the Garden of Eden they both can teach us many things. Sin of course has natural consequences that we put into motion when we decide, "God I think I know better than you do. Your commands are becoming quite outdated." If sickness hits us, through no fault of our own, Satan wants us to believe that we are helpless victims of our environment and our DNA. However, the truth is we may not be able to control getting a disease but we can always choose our response to that disease. I did not choose bipolar disorder, but every day I have a brand new opportunity to see how God has turned my story of brokenness into one of beauty.

God used Ronda to remind me that I could be a strong Christian and still have a mental health diagnosis. Being a Christian does not mean we do not have sins, sicknesses, or struggles. It does however mean we have a loving and all-powerful Savior who has promised to walk with us and carry us through each season of our lives.

Section 2

9

Neurotransmitters and Mental Health

Warning: This section may be slightly clinical!

Our brain is a fascinating organ made up of billions of neurons. Because of research we now know that what we often refer to as mental disorders are really brain disorders. The brain uses chemical messengers, called neurotransmitters, to communicate with other parts of itself and with our nervous system. Neurons, or nerve cells, communicate with each other by exchanging neurotransmitters. This way of communicating is how our brains function properly (Nemade, 2007).

Mental illness has been linked to problems in the brain with certain neurotransmitters such as serotonin, dopamine, norepinephrine, glutamate, and GABA (gamma-aminobutyric acid).

Let's begin with discussing the brain chemical, serotonin, which tends to be the most frequently talked about neurotransmitter. Serotonin, sometimes referred to as the "calming chemical" is believed to have an effect on maintaining our mood. Serotonin assists in regulating many essential bodily functions such as appetite, sleep, sexual behavior, and mood. Many experts believe that when serotonin in the brain is low it can cause an individual to feel depressed and even suicidal in some instances. Low serotonin can make it extremely difficult to control pessimistic thinking. For someone who has not experienced depression this is sometimes hard to understand. They would like to simply tell the depressed person to snap out of it and think more positively. This prescription for happiness may be easy for someone just having a bad day, but for someone with clinical depression it can be almost impossible.

There is some controversy between scientists whether decreased levels of serotonin contribute to depression or if depression causes levels in serotonin to decrease. Regardless of which hypothesis you believe, I think most of us would agree that increasing the brain's serotonin levels is bound to produce positive results. One natural way to increase serotonin levels in the brain is through regular exercise. Exercise has a similar effect on the brain as that of an anti-depressant.

Another neurotransmitter, which greatly affects our brain, is dopamine. Dopamine is often referred to as the "feel good" neurochemical. It helps control the brain's reward and pleasure centers and gives us clarity, sanity and soundness of mind. Dopamine imbalances have been linked to depression, binge eating, addiction, gambling, bipolar disorder, Alzheimer's, Parkinson's, schizophrenia, and ADHD.

If someone's dopamine levels get out of balance they may start to have hallucinations and delusions. An imbalance of dopamine can also cause extreme paranoia. Paranoia can lead people to believe that even their loved ones are out to harm them. In severe cases such as these, medication is almost always recommended as the treatment of choice. Paranoia has the ability to destroy great relationships. If someone is dealing with a dopamine imbalance and thinks others are against them they will most likely start accusing friends and family of doing things they did not do. When I was in the severity of bipolar disorder I began to believe that even Terrell was against me. I can only imagine how hurtful that must have been for him. He was my biggest advocate and was fighting for my healing and emotional stability, but until the medication was given the chance to balance out my brain chemicals it was difficult for me to know the truth-that he was wholeheartedly on my side. An imbalance of dopamine can cause you to feel like you are always looking over your shoulder and don't know who you can trust.

Norepinephrine, is another neurotransmitter that affects the brain, which in turn affects our everyday lives. Norepinephrine is the brain's version of adrenaline. It is responsible for helping us to be alert. When norepinephrine levels are in balance it mediates energy, a healthy libido, mental focus, and motivation. However, low norepinephrine can lead to lack of motivation, depression, fatigue, sexual dysfunction, and poor memory. When norepinephrine levels are too high it can lead to hypervigilance, insomnia, anxiety, and panic attacks.

Glutamate is the body's most prominent neurotransmitter, the brain's main excitatory neurotransmitter. Glutamate is believed to play a part in learning and memory. Depression and schizophrenia may stem from an inability of the central nervous system to utilize glutamate effectively (Dipardo, 2013).

Another chemical in our brain that directly affects our mental health is GABA (gamma-amino-butyric-acid). GABA is classified as an inhibitory neurotransmitter, as opposed to glutamate, which is an excitatory neurotransmitter. GABA helps us to not obsess over our worries, assists with sleep regulation, relaxation, and reduces physical pain. One of its functions is to control fear or anxiety that is experienced when neurons are overexcited. A deficiency in GABA may lead to many ailments such as depression, mood disorders, excessive stress, and insomnia.

Understanding how some of these neurotransmitters affect our brain can be beneficial in helping people with mental illness realize that having a mental disorder does not mean they have failed morally or they are mentally weak. A mental disorder is not a sign of inner weakness, but a sign that the brain's neurotransmitters may not be functioning optimally.

10

Major Depressive Disorder

Major Depressive Disorder, also known as Clinical Depression, affects more than 15 million adults in the United States in any given year. Research suggests it is caused by a combination of genetic, biological, environmental, and psychological factors. According to the National Institute of Mental Health (NIMH), Major Depressive Disorder (MDD) is the leading cause of disability in the United States for individuals ages 15-44. Clinical Depression is characterized by a variety of depressive symptoms lasting for at least 2 weeks.

Some symptoms of depression may include:

- Feelings of guilt, hopelessness, or worthlessness

- Difficulty concentrating, remembering, or making decisions

- Fatigue and lack of energy

- Loss of interest in activities that used to bring one pleasure

- Weight loss or weight gain

- Either insomnia or sleeping too much

- Restlessness or irritability

- Suicidal thoughts

In my own family, Clinical Depression is what caused my mom to abruptly quit her job as an elementary school teacher and to sink into such a dark place that at times she refused to leave the confines of home. The stigma from Depression is what kept her living and therefore hiding under a blanket of shame not wanting anyone to know what she was inwardly experiencing. My sister and I would come home from school and the house would be dark, and the curtains would be closed. It was painful to see her living that way and it affected us as well. Due to her Clinical Depression she was no longer comfortable driving and taking us places. When our friends would ask us to meet them at the mall we learned to make an excuse as to why we were unable to go. I never had the courage to say, "My mom suffers from Major Depressive Disorder and does not drive anymore. Can we get a ride from your mom or dad?"

In my estimation the shame that surrounds mental

illness is one of the worst parts of the disease. The individual who is suffering with depression often feels ashamed of their disease and feels they must hide it from family, friends, and co-workers. Add to that the confusion from outsiders, especially in the Body of Christ, and the embarrassment is only compounded. We must be careful to not be too quick to judge things we have not lived and that we may not understand. It is far too easy to simply tell someone to "pray and read your Bible" to overcome depression if you have never experienced it yourself. Some well-meaning Christians may even try and quote Scriptures to you while you are depressed. Nehemiah 8:10 says, "The joy of the Lord is your strength" and it is a popular verse often spoken to those who are in the midst of depression. Personally the Word of God has always brought me comfort and hope even when under distress in my mind. However, if it is used by a Christian to tell someone to only meditate on Scripture and not do anything else then it can become damaging. There were times when I heard messages that seemed to bring condemnation if you did not feel joy, because that must mean you did not trust God and therefore had sin in your life. This is not helpful. It is only harmful. There is a staunch difference between someone who needs to learn how to shake off self-pity and trust in God's joy to be their strength versus the person who lives with Major Depressive Disorder and needs medical intervention. We can no longer put those two different kinds of people in the same category and expect the same results from our messages on faith and joy.

There have been times I listened to preachers on television who are about to preach a message on joy begin their sermon with differentiating between struggling with occasional sadness versus clinical depression. These pastors bring a breath of fresh air. For someone like myself who has battled immense feelings of guilt at times for taking psychiatric medications, hearing a pastor recognize the difference between sadness and clinical depression allowed me the space I needed to exhale and feel okay about myself. I only wish I had heard it more often. I came to realize that most people who speak from the pulpit about depression or mental health only speak from what they have heard and not from what they have experienced. There were a few years when I was not on any psychiatric medications and I believed I had been supernaturally healed. I gave my testimony a few times during those years and wonder if I made comments that made other people feel like their healing was not as legitimate if they were on medication, since during that time I was not. This is potentially detrimental to our faith to assume that God must heal the same way in every situation.

Let us take a look at a few different healings in the Bible. Jesus healed people in a variety of ways. Sometimes He would simply speak a word and they were healed. Another time He challenged a man with a shriveled hand to stretch it out (Luke 6:6-10). Jesus even spit on the ground once, made mud with his saliva, and told a man born blind to wash in the Pool of Siloam (John 9). Had I lived in Bible days I think I would have asked Jesus to simply speak a word for me to be healed. "Please don't put mud and spit on my eyes, Lord!" But Jesus heals how He chooses. It is only my pride that would not have wanted mud on my eyes. "What will my friends and other

> *I know God has a plan for my life that is different than anyone else's and He simply asks me to trust Him.*

church leaders say?" However, God in his Sovereignty will always take us back to a place of child-like faith if we allow Him.

I do not understand why my mom was instantaneously healed one day and why my journey has had many ups and downs, but I do know this, that God loves and cherishes me as much as He does my mom. I know

God has a plan for my life that is different than anyone else's and He simply asks me to trust Him. Jeremiah 29:11 powerfully proclaims that God has plans for each of us to prosper us and give us a great hope and future. When I stop to look around and compare my journey with someone else's I will never find the complete freedom that God has waiting for me. This is why childlike faith and trust is an essential part of this Christian life.

In the Bible, even the disciples compared their life journey to those of their fellow disciples. Simon Peter was notorious for this in John 21:21. Jesus had already died on the cross, risen from the dead, and was now spending some much needed quality time with Peter. Peter had recently denied Jesus and now Jesus was reinstating him by having Peter reaffirm his love and faith in His Lord.

The story continues in John 21:18 – 19 when Jesus says:

I tell you the truth, when you were younger you dressed yourself and went where you wanted, but when you are old you will stretch out your hands, and someone else will dress you and lead you where you do not want to go. Jesus said this to indicate the kind of death by which Peter would glorify God. Then he said to him, 'Follow me!'

The next couple verses are quite humorous if you picture the scene. Jesus had just finished having this deep conversation with Peter about love and feeding his sheep. He had also very poetically declared to Peter how he would die. Instead of Peter asking his Lord for strength to endure death or for more insight on how to feed Jesus' sheep he looks around and finds John. It is not enough for Peter to be convinced that Jesus will be with him when he goes through these difficult things, he wants to know "what about him Lord?"

Many of us can probably see ourselves in Peter. God is actively taking care of us and seeking to speak to our hearts, but maybe my story does not look like your story and so I fall straight into the trap of comparison. "Lord," I might say, "what about my friend who has never dealt with depression, anxiety, or bipolar symptoms a day in her life. Her life seems perfect and that is not fair Lord!" When I fall into this trap I take my eyes off my Lord. We must realize that when we take our eyes off the Lord and look around we will inevitably begin to sink. We will sink lower into a pit of despair and self-pity. Comparison is a weapon used by Satan to convince us that God has forgotten about us or He must not truly love us the way He loves our friends. If you have ever felt this way then I encourage you to fight back with the Word of God and scriptures such as, Jeremiah 29:11, "For I know the plans I have for you," declares the Lord, "plans to prosper you and not to harm you, plans to give you hope and a future."

We can no longer pretend that as Christians our problems are different from the problems in the world. Our problems are identical many times. The difference is we have an eternal hope and have put our trust in Jesus Christ. However, knowing this does not make someone's clinical depression disappear. There are practical steps to take that can help facilitate healing. Please see the chapter on *8 Healthy Habits for a Healthy Life* and remember that whether or not your healing comes supernaturally, gradually, or with the assistance of medication does not define who you are. I no longer tell God how He needs to heal me. He has healed me through allowing me to live a productive life and be proactive about my mental health, whether that includes taking medication or not. If you allow your story to touch others and you fight for yourself and your health, then you are walking in healing and wholeness every day. Accept that and refuse to compare your story or your journey with that of anyone else.

11

Anxiety Disorders

Anxiety disorders are the most common of mental health issues in the United States and affect approximately 40 million adults, which is about 18% of the population. According to the Anxiety and Depression Association of America (ADAA), it is especially common for someone who suffers with depression to also suffer with anxiety and vice versa. Approximately half of those diagnosed with an anxiety disorder are also diagnosed with depression.

Anxiety is a normal reaction to stressful situations and everyone experiences some form of anxiety at times. However, for those who have an anxiety disorder, anxiety becomes excessive and negatively interferes with their daily living. There are a variety of anxiety disorders such as; Generalized Anxiety Disorder, Panic Disorder, Social Anxiety Disorder, Post-Traumatic Stress Disorder, Obsessive-Compulsive Disorder, and Specific Phobias.

I want to focus on Generalized Anxiety Disorder (GAD)

which affects 6.8 million adults or 3.1% of the United States population. Generalized Anxiety Disorder is characterized by at least 6 months of excessive and persistent anxiety and/or worry. Some of the symptoms may include:

- Difficulty concentrating

- Irritability or restlessness

- Persistent worry

- Fatigue/exhaustion

- Muscle tension

- Difficulty falling asleep or staying asleep

Although I was never formally diagnosed with an anxiety disorder I have personally experienced symptoms of anxiety that were so intense that it affected my regular day to day functioning. Growing up I remember being an anxious child starting around the age of ten. I think I may have hid it pretty well, but there were times of excessive worry beyond what I would consider to be within normal limits.

I was an extremely conscientious child growing up. For example, although I never forgot my homework I would at times anxiously obsess and think, "What if I forget my homework?" I was also hyperaware and wanted to be sure that no one else, especially my mom worried about me forgetting things. Although unsolicited, I would at times go over my mental checklist with her out loud before school. I would say, "Mom, just so you know I have my homework, my lunch, eyeglasses, and school supplies." As I got older it seems that I outgrew some of the anxiousness temporarily.

Although I did experience some anxiety in college it was manageable most of the time. However, there was one year in college around the time of final exams when I broke out with an ugly rash. I went to the school nurse who diagnosed me with hives although she could not figure out the source. She said maybe it was something I ate. I did not figure it out until years later that there was a direct correlation in my outbreak of hives and my increased anxiety around final exams. Every year in college I did well, but sometimes around finals the thought would come, "What if I don't do well this year?" Anxiety is an expert at asking all the "what if" questions. I now like to challenge myself as well as my clients to turn it back around and say, "What if I do extremely well and everything works out just fine?" Sometimes we have to look anxiety and worry straight in the eye and choose to believe that we can do whatever we think we cannot do, and believe we will overcome whatever the obstacle might be.

About five years after being diagnosed with bipolar disorder I became aware of what had the potential to trigger anxiety for me. It seemed if I was in an unfamiliar situation and was not feeling confident it could trigger debilitating anxiety. There was a time when I changed job positions and decided to try my hand at teaching pre-kindergarten (pre-k). Since my Bachelor's degree was not in elementary education the licensing board approved me to begin teaching on a provisional license as long as I attended Saturday classes to receive my certification to teach pre-k. Looking back none of that seems frightening or intimidating now, but at the time I felt extremely overwhelmed on a daily basis. I remember speaking to my supervisor about my doubts in my own ability to handle the necessary requirements. She believed in my ability and was tremendously supportive. She assured me that she would help walk me through each step of the process. However, due to my severe anxiety at the time I did not believe in myself the way she believed in me. One day, after being fed up with all the anxiety I was experiencing I called her and told her I was sorry but I would not be returning. I felt tremendous embarrassment and an overwhelming sense of shame in quitting my job so abruptly. However, the increasing anxiety I felt on a daily basis was even greater than my fear of embarrassment and shame.

Living with anxiety can be debilitating at times. It can make you feel paralyzed and doing even small things at times seems like a major undertaking. There is often a lot of second-guessing of oneself if you are experiencing anxiety and you struggle to feel confident in yourself or your abilities. Fear seems to overtake you and you find it difficult to shake those feelings of anxiety and insecurity.

Treatment normally consists of psychotherapy and medication, including anti-depressants. For those who would like to consider other options as well there are many natural ways to start to combat anxiety. Other than the *8 Healthy Habits* mentioned toward the end of this book, some other treatment options for anxiety are as follows.

Progressive Muscle Relaxation - Many times anxiety causes your body to carry a great deal of muscle tension. This can lead to aches and pains, and also leave you feeling exhausted emotionally, mentally, and physically. Progressive Muscle Relaxation (PMR) teaches how to intentionally focus on tensing and then relaxing one muscle at a time. *If you have a history of injuries, please consult your doctor before you begin.*

The best way to start PMR is to get comfortable and relaxed in a quiet environment. Focus on inhaling during the tension phase and then exhaling while you are relaxing each muscle group. I recommend systematically starting with your feet and working your way all the way up toward your face. You may want to say the word "tense" before you tense each muscle group and hold it for five seconds. Then say the word, "Relax" and abruptly relax that muscle, not gradually. Then hold the relaxation phase for a count of ten. It is often helpful to rate your anxiety level on a scale of 1-10 before PMR and again afterward. Below is an example:

Relaxation sequence:

Feet – Curl your toes downwards.

Lower legs – Point your toes toward your face. Do this slowly and carefully to avoid cramps.

Thighs – Clench them hard.

Buttocks – Squeeze buttocks together tightly.

Chest and stomach – Suck stomach into a tight knot.

Back – Arch your back and pretend you are going to let your shoulder blades touch each other.

Shoulders – Tense your shoulders as you raise them toward your ears.

Neck – Be gentle with the neck muscles. Turn slowly to

the right and hold the tension and then turn toward the left and hold the tension.

Upper arms- One arm at a time, bring your forearm to your shoulder as if to "make a muscle."

Hands and forearms – Make a fist with each hand.

Forehead – Raise your eyebrows as high as you can.

Eyes and cheeks – Squeeze your eyes tightly shut.

Mouth – Open your mouth wide as if you are yawning.

Jaw – Make a wide smile.

Praise & Worship – This treatment method may not be found in many books but it is something I have discovered is soothing to my soul. Psalm 8:2 declares, "Through the praise of children and infants you have established a stronghold against your enemies, to silence the foe and the avenger." There is something that happens in the atmosphere when we start to worship God. It shifts our focus from our anxiety and worries onto His goodness and faithfulness. Praise silences the lies of the Enemy.

In the middle of my stays in and out of the psychiatric hospital, God impressed on Terrell's heart to play praise and worship music 24 hours a day in the house. I remember coming home and hearing it quietly playing in the background and it brought such peace to my soul.

Paying Attention – In our modern era where we each hold miniature computers in the palm of our hands (cellphones), it is possible to never be quiet and to always be staring at a screen. The news is readily available, as is all forms of entertainment. Since we are the gatekeepers of our

> *We cannot pray for peace from God and then not use the wisdom of God.*

souls we must begin to pay attention to what we are watching, reading, and listening to. We cannot pray for peace from God and then not use the wisdom of God. Some shows on television may be captivating and interesting but if you know it could potentially cause anxiety, then have the self-control to turn it off. This can make a major difference in your anxiety levels.

12

Bipolar Disorder

Bipolar Disorder (previously known as manic-depression) affects approximately 3% of the American population and can feel like having two illnesses at the same time. It is a brain disorder that causes unusual shifts in mood, activity levels, and energy. People who have bipolar disorder experience periods called "mood episodes." These are not to be confused with regular mood swings, which, at times, everyone experiences. The mood fluctuations associated with Bipolar Disorder are much more severe in nature and include extreme disturbances in the person's activity level, energy, and sleep patterns. Sometimes a mood episode includes both symptoms of mania and depressive symptoms and this is referred to as a "mixed episode."

According to psychosis-bipolar.com, "In 60% to 70% of the persons affected, the bipolar disease commences with a depressive episode; accordingly in 20% to 30% with a manic episode." However, many individuals living with bipolar disorder report that in retrospect they had already began to feel different in their mood or behavior before they received a medical diagnosis of Bipolar Disorder. These symptoms can be referred to as early warning symptoms. Listed below are some early warning symptoms of depression and mania.

Possible early warning symptoms of depression:

- Tiredness and lack of energy

- Reduced self-confidence

- Increased anxiety and worry

- Depressed mood

- Sleep disturbances

- Concentration difficulties

- Reduced sexual interest

- Decrease in productivity

- Lack of interest in pleasurable activities

- Changes in the normal routine

- Irritability

Possible early warning symptoms of mania:

- Feelings of euphoria or elation

- Racing thoughts

- Increased need to talk

- Increased energy and activity level

- Decreased need for sleep

- Increased self-confidence or feelings of importance

- Irritability and impatience

- Increased sexual interest

- Increased desire to spend money

- Concentration difficulties, easily distractible

- Agitation, restlessness

- Increased alcohol/drug consumption

Under the umbrella of Bipolar Disorder are Bipolar I disorder, Bipolar II Disorder, and Cyclothymic Disorder. Each of these basic types of bipolar disorder include clear disturbances in mood, energy, and activity level. These moods range from periods of feeling euphoric and energized (known as a manic episode) to periods of extreme sadness and hopelessness (known as a depressive episode). Less severe manic periods are referred to as hypomanic episodes.

According to the National Institute of Mental Health website (Nimh.nih.Gov)

Bipolar I Disorder – defined by manic episodes that may last at least seven days, or by manic symptoms that are severe enough that the person needs hospitalization. Usually, depressive episodes occur as well, typically lasting at least two weeks. Periods of depression and manic symptoms occurring at the same time are referred to as a mixed episode.

Bipolar II Disorder – defined by a pattern of depressive episodes and hypomanic episodes, but not full-blown manic episodes.

Cyclothymic Disorder (also called cyclothymia)– defined by numerous periods of hypomanic symptoms as well as numerous periods of depressive symptoms lasting for at least two years (one year in children and adolescents). However, the symptoms do not meet the diagnostic criteria for a hypomanic episode and a depressive episode.

Individuals with all forms of bipolar disorder can live successful and productive lives. An effective treatment plan will usually combine psychotherapy (also known as "talk therapy") and medication. It is extremely important for someone with bipolar disorder to track his or her moods on a consistent basis. If you have a mental illness, make the brave decision to not allow it to destroy your life. I challenge you to become an active participant in your treatment which enables you to no longer feel like a victim at the mercy of a diagnosis, but enables you to become an active participant on your journey of wholeness.

13

Suicidal Ideation

What is suicidal ideation? Suicidal ideation is merely a clinical term for suicidal thoughts. Suicidal ideation can vary from passing thoughts about ending one's life to a detailed plan with how and when one will end his or her life. Whether these thoughts are passing or planned out they need to be discussed and brought out into the open.

Suicidal warning signs may include:

- Isolation and withdrawing from social contact

- Being preoccupied with death and dying

- Feeling trapped or hopeless

- Giving away belongings and getting affairs in order

- Increased use of alcohol or drugs

- Changes in mood and/or behavior

- Talking about not wanting to live

- Obtaining items needed for suicide attempt

- Participating in reckless behavior

- Aggressive behavior

- Suddenly becoming calm after a period of moodiness can be a sign that the person has made the decision to end his or her life

Suicide happens when people feel they are completely without hope. There is probably not one person who will read this that has not been affected by someone taking his or her life. These loved ones are sometimes referred to as Suicide Survivors. I have been personally affected by this. I have a family member who became overwhelmed with mental suffering and ended his life. I also have close friends who have lost loved ones because of suicide. This is a pain from which you never completely recover. It is almost impossible to not ask yourself, "Could I have prevented this from happening?" If you blame yourself for a loved one's suicide I would recommend talking to a Mental Health Professional about these painful feelings.

Here are some possible effects upon the Suicide Survivors:

- Deep depression and feelings of hopelessness

- Attempting to relive the last moments with their loved one to figure out how they could have prevented it

- Anger

- Shame

- Guilt

- Complicated grief, partly due to the stigma associated with suicide

The fact remains that although we cannot bring back our loved one, we can be diligent to make certain the life they lived helps others.

If you are suffering with thoughts of suicide, remember that as long as there is breath in your body there is hope. If you are reading this as a person who struggles with suicidal thoughts know that at times those thoughts seem so real and true, but they are not. They are lies from the Evil One. Stop and think about what you are telling yourself. If you are telling yourself that your family would be better off without you, please know that is a false belief. You are in control of the movie you allow to play on the screen of your mind.

My beautiful mother, began believing this lie when she was suffering with severe depression. She thought my sister and I would be better off without her. What a lie that was! I cannot imagine if she would have chosen to end her life those many years ago. At the time she thought she would always be in a deep, dark, pit. She did not know that God was going to bring her out of despair and heal her and set her free, but He did. She has now been free from depression for 15 years! What if in a moment of temporary pain, weakness, and isolation she would have given up hope and convinced herself that life without her would be better? My sister and I, and all our family and friends would have been left to suffer, left to pick up the broken pieces and deal with grief we would have known was avoidable.

It is excruciating enough to deal with normal grief. However, the grief due to suicide is a complicated kind of grief. This grief leaves the family and friends with undeniable guilt. It makes the children ask the painful question, "How could I have not been enough to keep my mommy or daddy alive?" If you are thinking of suicide please reach out to a loved one NOW or call the suicide hotline number at 1-800-SUICIDE or 1-800-273-8255.

Some people are afraid to ask their depressed loved ones if they have ever thought of hurting themselves or ending their life. Many times the loved one will say, "I do not want to put that thought in their head." However, that is simply not the case. If someone is not considering suicide then you asking them about it is not going to make them begin to contemplate it. We have to be courageous enough to ask our family and friends who are suffering with mental illness if they have thought of hurting themselves. Depression, bipolar disorder, schizophrenia, and other mental illnesses can become quite a scary place in the mind of the person suffering. Living with these secret thoughts of no longer wanting to live is frightening to say the least. When life gets dark, discussing the darkness actually brings it into the light.

I have learned that Satan does his best work in dark secrecy. When we bring it to light, we bind him up. Let us begin the conversation when we know it could be necessary. It is literally a matter of life and death.

Section 3

14

8 Healthy Habits for a Healthy Life

Everyone, whether diagnosed with a mental disorder or not needs to learn how to incorporate healthy self-care into his or her daily life. After I was released from the hospital I found a therapist who I really connected with and she continued to remind me about self-care and the importance of establishing healthy habits. Dictionary.com simply defines a habit as, "An acquired behavior pattern regularly followed until it has become almost involuntary." It can also be defined as a "customary practice." Each of us must ask the question, "What are my acquired patterns or my customary practices?" These practices that we participate in on a consistent basis can either help our lives to become successful or will lead us down a path of destructiveness. The choice belongs completely to us.

Some of these healthy habits I believe are essential are:

1. Positive Self-Talk and Power Thoughts

Although I did not write these *8 Healthy Habits* in any particular order, this one would definitely be among my top three. I have personally tested this habit and it is absolutely true! What is amazing to me is the fact that the secular world is finally catching up to what the Bible taught approximately 2,000 years ago.

Around 62 A.D. the Apostle Paul wrote in Philippians 4:8:

Finally, brethren, whatever things are true, whatever things are honest, whatever things are just, whatever things are pure, whatever things are lovely, whatever things are of good report; if there is any virtue, and if there is anything praiseworthy, meditate on these things.

The things we choose to mediate on and focus on in our lives will have a direct effect on our moods and our attitudes. The days that I have chosen to think negatively or to have my very own pity-party are the days that I have felt equally down in the dumps. However, the days where I have had a grateful heart and mind are the days where joy seems to come more freely. Please know I am not suggesting that if you are clinically depressed you only need to change your thoughts and all the chemicals in your brain will magically change, but I am saying that we have to work with our brain and not against it.

I believe the best prescription for clinical depression is finding a great Christian counselor, getting on the medication that you and your doctor decide is best for you, and adding these healthy habits to your life as well.

Be sure that every day you wake up you are telling yourself the truth. Telling yourself the truth can be the catalyst for your healing. The truth of my life is that yes, I was diagnosed with bipolar disorder in 1998, and I did consider it unfair. I was 23 years old and confused and felt abandoned by God, but He has taken the pain of my life and turned it into purpose to help other people.

Proverbs 23:7 (NKJV) says, "For as he thinks in his heart so is he." I never realized the amazing power of our thoughts until the last few years. In my practice as a Licensed Professional Counselor I have seen many different people who are experiencing similar situations. It is remarkable how a variety of individuals can all experience very similar events and yet be affected so completely differently. Many factors contribute to this phenomenon, but it most often comes down to their thought life and what they are telling themselves about their situation.

2. Find your Tribe

In Genesis 2:18 after God created Adam He said, "It is not good for the man to be alone. I will make a helper suitable for him." It is fascinating that God said it is not good for man to be alone. However, Adam was not literally alone. He had the Creator of the Universe with whom to talk and fellowship. But God in His ultimate wisdom knew that would not be enough to meet all of Adam's emotional needs. Adam needed someone who was His equal to talk with and fellowship with. Whether you are married or single, you must find people who you connect with and who you can have healthy and transparent fellowship. Isolation is one of the number one traps of the enemy, especially if you are going through a mental health crisis. Satan wants to convince you that no one understands what you are going through. If he can convince you of that then your distress will only worsen. This is why it is essential to stay connected to people, regardless of how you might feel. I look at the life of Jesus and how the multitudes and the crowds would follow Him. Yet Jesus poured His life into the 12 disciples and even out of that He had a more intimate relationship with the three; Peter, James, and John. Do you have three intimate friends that you could call any time of day or night? If you do that is fantastic, but if you do not then it is time to be intentional about making yourself friendlier. Proverbs 18:24a (NKJV) says, "A man who has friends must himself be friendly." Take a risk and visit churches in your area that have small groups with people who are in a similar stage of life as you are or consider joining a book club at your local library. There are multiple ways to begin meeting like-minded people but it may take some persistence and intentionality. Be willing to not give up until you have found your tribe!

3. Be Assertive and Set Proper Boundaries

Learning to be assertive and knowing how to set proper boundaries can be the difference between emotional stability and mental instability. Setting boundaries is invaluable in numerous situations. I know many people, women in particular who are frustrated, stressed, and on the verge of burn out simply because they have not learned how to say "no". The word *no* really can be the most anointed word you will ever learn to say. Each time you say "yes" when you know you should have said "no" a little seed of resentment is planted in your soul. You may not realize it at the time, but later as time passes and more seeds of resentment are planted and then watered by regret that you said yes, may start you to wondering how you became so bitter. When we ignore the voice of the Holy Spirit telling us to say no to something, and because of guilt or manipulation we say yes anyway it will eventually turn you into a person you never wanted to be. Please realize that only you can determine what is right for you at each season of life. If you choose to strive to live up to other people's expectations of you, you will be most miserable. The only life worth living is yours! And the only person who can control what you do is you. People may try to control you through guilt and manipulation but you alone must choose whether or not to get on that roller coaster of people pleasing.

I like to picture people pleasing like a ride at an amusement park. It will take you up high when you do what they want and will drop you down very low if you do not succumb to their

> *The only life worth living is yours!*

expectation of what they want you to be or do. The next time you find yourself about to follow someone onto that roller coaster ride of people pleasing realize you have the power to stay on the platform and refuse to take a ride on the people pleasing roller coaster. Learning to set proper boundaries is essential if you truly desire to be the person God has called you to be. You will never be all you were called to be by chasing after the approval of people. I highly recommend Henry Cloud and John Townsend's book, Boundaries, if you are struggling with guilt whenever you say no, or if you are a person who rarely says no because feeling guilty is too overwhelming. Remember, we teach people how to treat us. No one can operate control over your life if you do not allow them.

4. *Move Your Body*

Any regimen of healthy self-care must include some form of regular exercise. The type of exercise you engage in is completely up to you but you must be intentional about moving your body and getting your heart rate elevated on a regular basis. Research has proven that exercise raises levels of serotonin in the brain just like SSRI anti-depressant medications do. For someone who suffers with only mild depression sometimes regular exercise proves to be all they need to raise their serotonin levels enough to come out of depression. Of course the quandary occurs often because most people who are depressed do not have the motivation to get up and exercise. This is when your will-power must kick in. The times when I have been in a depression sometimes going to the gym was all I did that entire day, but something inside me told myself I had to do at least that. Love yourself enough to not allow yourself to slip into a darker place than you may already be in.

This was one stark difference between my mother and me. Her bouts with depression were so dark that she did not leave the house and she was getting no exercise whatsoever. Although I have had bouts of depression, mine never got to the place where I was confining myself to the house. Knowing the necessity of walking around the block or paying for a monthly gym membership can mean the difference between a life worth living and a life lived in isolation. Refuse to be the person who lives in isolation regardless of how you feel. This is where *positive self-talk and power thoughts* come into play. You may think you hate exercise but I want you to start saying out loud, "I love to exercise and move my body every day." When you realize that exercise can change your outlook on life you will be more prone to do it. Find a form of exercise that you enjoy and refuse to compare your level of fitness with anyone else's.

Personally, I enjoy group fitness classes. There have been many times when I have gone to the gym, looked around, and realized I am the most out of shape person in the class. The temptation is to engage in negative self-talk, but I have learned I must talk back to myself in a positive voice. The inner conversation may go like this, "Tara, it does not matter if everyone in here looks like an athlete and you do not. What matters is that you showed up! You are not competing against anyone else. You are here for you." A good old-fashioned pep talk can be enough to encourage you to stay in the game. Comparison will lower your self-esteem and make you want to head for the nearest exit. I have noticed a direct correlation in my life and in the lives of my clients. When my *comparison* of myself to other people increases, my personal *confidence* decreases. It is directly correlated. Do not allow yourself to wish you looked like or had the personality of anyone else. God has made and designed you to be uniquely you!

It is time to be confident in who you were created to be. If you struggle with that then it is past time for you to learn to fight back against those negative voices. Find positive people to surround yourself with or

> *When my comparison of myself to other people increases, my personal confidence decreases.*

to listen to online and build yourself up inwardly. What you deposit in your soul will come out in the life you live! Every choice you make whether it is moving your body, feeding yourself healthy food, or listening to positive people online will manifest itself in your outer life. Take the time necessary to develop yourself to be the person you want to be.

If you are a person who has to fight to remember that you are worth fighting for then I encourage you to read Psalm 139 aloud daily to remind yourself that God created you especially unique.

Psalm 139:13-16 says:

For you created my inmost being; you knit me together in my mother's womb. I praise you because I am fearfully and wonderfully made; your works are wonderful, I know that full well. My frame was not hidden from you when I was made in the secret place, when I was woven together in the depths of the earth.

Your eyes saw my unformed body; all the days ordained for me were written in your book before one of them came to be.

> *What you deposit in your soul will come out in the life you live!*

5. Release Fear

II Timothy 1:7 (Amplified) says:

For God did not give us a spirit of timidity (of cowardice, of craven and cringing and fawning fear), but [He has given us a spirit] of power and of love and of a calm and well-balanced mind and discipline and self-control.

The best acronym I have ever heard for FEAR is *False Evidence Appearing Real.* One of Satan's greatest weapons is fear. He knows that if he can get us to be afraid then we will not fulfill the purpose and destiny God has called us to. John 10:10 (Amplified) reminds us, "The thief comes only in order to steal and kill and destroy. I came that they may have and enjoy life, and have it in abundance (to the full, till it overflows)." The fear that Satan likes to threaten us with will attempt to steal, kill, and destroy our destiny and purpose. We were each called for a divine purpose. If there is breath in your body then God has work for you to do. Satan desires that we shrink back from that purpose. He will tell us lies about ourselves or remind us of the reasons we are unqualified to fulfill God's purpose for our life. Sometimes people will tell me that they feel they are not good enough to do what God has called them to do. And they are right! You, nor I, will ever be good enough to fulfill God's purpose. That is why Jesus had to come to earth and shed His blood so we can now declare that we have His righteousness. I am grateful that it does not depend on me. The confidence that we are all searching for must come from knowing that without Jesus we will continue to feel insignificant and worthless. However, when you have asked Jesus to be in your life He chases away the insecurity if we allow Him to.

Two fears that Satan uses to plague people are the fear of failure and the fear of success. The fear of failure is more commonly discussed. Many are afraid that if they try something new they might not succeed at it. The first day I went back to school to obtain my master's degree in counseling I felt an overwhelming sense of fear. At the time I did not even know how to send an attachment through an e-mail. I knew the majority of my coursework was going to have to be submitted online and fear consumed me. "What if I can't do it?" I questioned. I had been out of college for 10 years and the thought of having to study for exams and write papers again was intimidating. The Enemy is very adept at reminding you of why you cannot succeed and why you should not even attempt to break out of your comfort zone. "Who do you think you are to attempt to start a business, write a book, go back to school?" I think of a graveyard and how that is the most fertile soil on the planet. I do not want to die with seeds of greatness inside me that I never watered or allowed to grow.

Compared to eternity, life is truly short. The average life span in the United States is approximately 78 years. That is not even a drop in the bucket compared to eternity. May the cry of our heart be to stand before God one day and hear Him say, "Well done, good and faithful servant" (Luke 19:17). There is nothing I want to hear more. Be willing to take risks. Be willing to look foolish. If you stay in your comfort zone you will never grow. Determine to be a person who would rather take a risk and fail than never risk at all. Failing forward is powerful. Each time we try something new we are building our inner muscles of strength and courage. Every time we get back up after we fall down it is like we are building new muscle fibers of inner strength. Proverbs 24:16a says, "For though the righteous fall seven times, they rise again."

What about those who fear success? This is an adage not often talked about. We declare we want to be successful, but some people have an inward inferiority complex and do not believe they deserve to achieve success. However, I want to redefine what I believe success truly is. Success is being right in the center of God's will for your life. This will look differently for each one of us. By this definition, the missionary in a foreign country with an underground church of twenty people who has been called there by God is just as successful as the pastor called by God to be on television and pastor a church of 10,000 members. It all comes down to obedience.

> *Success is being right in the center of God's will for your life.*

Our obedience to the Lord is

what makes us successful. 1 Samuel 15:22 (NASB) demonstrates this clearly when Samuel says to Saul, "Has the Lord as much delight in burnt offerings and sacrifices as in obeying the voice of the Lord?"

While we are aware that we no longer need to offer burnt sacrifices to the Lord, I believe there is still so much present-day wisdom packed into this short verse. Our life's work should not be based upon sacrificing and doing more if God has not called us to do that. This truth came alive to me during my college years. Like many students at Oral Roberts University, I had great, big dreams and ambitions of all I wanted to do for God someday. Then one day a chapel speaker came and shook up my less than perfect inward motivation. He looked at us and said, "Are you willing to say yes to God regardless of what He asks you to do or where He asks you to go?"

The chapel speaker talked to us that day about how great it is to have ambition, but will we allow our ambition to outdo our obedience? I started to ask myself the hard questions. Would I obey God if He called me to pastor a church in a small town one day where no one would ever know my name? The Spirit of God came over me in that moment and I began to weep with brokenness. I knew my motivation for serving God had not been completely pure. I did not want God to call me to serve Him in what I considered a small way, in possibly a small church located in a small town. I wanted to do big things for God!

Of course serving God in a *big* way is great if that is what He has called you or me to do. But will we commit to obey Him no matter how big or small the

> *God will honor our simple obedience to Him more than our extravagant ambition.*

task? God will honor our simple obedience to Him more than our extravagant ambition.

6. Decrease Your Stress by Increasing Your Joy

Life can definitely be filled to the brim with stress. We must take mental inventory of everything we are doing in our lives and ask is this the season for me to be dedicating the time and energy necessary for this task? If we do not stop and ask ourselves this question then our lives will start to feel like a chaotic mess. It is never beneficial to get to the point where it feels like life is dragging you around by your fingernails and you are barely hanging on. You are the CEO of your life and must use the wisdom you have been given from the Holy Spirit to take charge of your schedule. There will be times when more of your life is dictated to you than you would like because of uncontrollable and temporary circumstances. However, when those seasons drag on for too long it is time to stop and reevaluate.

What are the non-negotiables in your life and then what are those things that can be changed? Only you can make the decision to change your schedule. Most people will consume as much of your time as you allow. Sometimes we do not say "no" because we are afraid of what others will think of us or that we won't appear as nice and loving Christians. Other times we refuse to say "no" to other people's requests and expectations because deep down we have inferiority issues. We are afraid of feeling less than someone else so we will work ourselves to exhaustion to prove our adequacy and self-worth. As long as our self-worth is founded on anything other than the work of Jesus it will never be enough and we will never feel like we are enough. Regularly take inventory and ask, "Where is my adequacy coming from? What is keeping me propped up?"

When anxiety seeps in what are the thoughts that go with it? Sometimes it is strongly connected to the comparison trap. The comparison trap says, "Look at what that person over there is doing. They are such a great parent, teacher, ministry leader, etc." Each of us can fill in the blank with our own varied sense of insecurity and comparison.

Hebrews 10:35 (Amplified) clearly admonishes, "Do not, therefore, fling away your fearless confidence, for it carries great and glorious compensation of reward." There will be some days when you feel more confident than others. Realize that no one on the planet feels confident all the time and in every situation. Confidence is fluid and sometimes feels like a wave in the ocean, other times like a bubbling brook, and at times like a dry desert. Realizing that truth can help us stop comparing ourselves to others. When planning your schedule refuse to say, "But that

> *Confidence is fluid and sometimes feels like a wave in the ocean, other times like a bubbling brook, and at times like a dry desert.*

person seems to have it all together and why can't I?" You were made to be you and you will never be good at fulfilling someone else's destiny. If you do not make the necessary adjustments to your schedule you will find yourself dry spiritually and eventually void of joy.

7. God Time

An essential aspect of healthy self-care must include personal one-on-one time with your Creator. One thing you will learn the longer you live is that the busyness of life never slows down if we do not intentionally make it slow down. Many times we speak of having time, talents, and treasure to offer to the Lord. Out of these three gifts only one of them is exactly equal for each of us, and that is the gift of time. We all have different talents, various levels of wealth (treasure), but each of us regardless of our socio-economic status or our giftedness is given 24 hours a day, which is equivalent to 1,440 minutes or 86,400 seconds per day. What will we do with the time we have been given? Will we stop and settle ourselves down and carve out some of that to spend alone with God?

In Mark 6:31 Jesus' disciples had just returned from their first preaching assignment. They had been doing the work of the Lord and were excited to tell Him all they had done for him and for the kingdom. Jesus allowed them to share but then said to them, "Come with me by yourselves to a quiet place and get some rest" (Mark 6:31). I love this about Jesus. He knew they were ambitious and had had a great adventure already, but He also recognized their need for some quiet time with Him. If we allow it, the demands of life will fill up every second of our day. Remarkably, even after Jesus said this the crowds still followed them so their quiet time was cut short. We can all relate to that with social media and modern technology. If we do not decide to unplug from the demands of life we can go weeks and months without spending quiet time alone with our Maker. We must realize that He knows our schedules and the demands on our time. He does something miraculous when we set aside our *to-do list* to spend time in prayer or in His Word. He is able to multiply that time back to us. I have seen Him do this for me on many occasions, but I think the temptation will always be there for us to take care of our daily demands first and then give God the leftovers of our time. What might happen if we prioritized our time with Him and then invited him to help us get everything else on our list accomplished?

8. *Discover Your Purpose*

After having been diagnosed with bipolar disorder in 1998 and feeling like I was floundering in terms of discovering purpose I remember attending a church one Friday night where the lady there prophetically told me, "Young lady you are mining in the wrong field." She did not know me and said this prompted by the Spirit of God. I left church that night frustrated and discouraged. At the time I was a teacher's assistant and had not seriously sought after God in terms of my specific purpose. My husband had been a Music Pastor at different churches and we knew one day we would found our own church, but in the meantime I did not know what God had truly called me to do. When she said I was mining in the wrong field part of me wanted to stay frustrated that God would have her give me a "word from the Lord" with no specific direction to come alongside it. I probably pouted and whined to the Lord for a few days, but then I decided to start to actively seek God concerning His will for my life. "What is my specific purpose?" I wrote in my journal that evening. I heard nothing but silence. And so this prayer continued for about a month, "God show me my destiny! Show me my purpose!" Almost a month to the day when I first wrote the prayer in my journal I was on the elliptical at the gym with my earplugs in watching television. Out of nowhere I heard the voice of God speak to my heart and simply say, "Counseling." All of a sudden I knew God had spoken to me! He wanted me to go back to school for counseling. Maybe He was going to take the brokenness of my story and turn it into something to help others. I was suddenly filled with purpose. God did have a plan for my life. I went home that day and began to research different schools where I could go to obtain my master's degree in professional counseling. God opened up every door but it was not without self-doubt, fear, and anxiety. The first day of online classes I thought I was going to have a panic attack. Fear gripped my heart. "I don't even know how to send an attachment through an email," I told my husband. "How will I be able to attend school online?" But because I was a mom and still holding down a full-time job I knew going to a classroom a few nights a week was unrealistic for me. In the middle of my doubts and thoughts of quitting before I began; I called my friend, Angela, and poured out to her all my doubts and fear of failure. She prayed with me and before we got off the phone she said, "Tara, I started school today too." Now it was my turn to pray for her. That is what having a tribe can do for you! When you are weak that other person can help support you and vice versa.

I do not want to give the impression that I never had another doubt or fear after that day, but God always showed up when I invited him into the doubts of my heart. One time when I was struggling with all the assignments and exams, He again showed up and spoke quietly but firmly to my heart. God said, "Take it one day at a time." This was something I knew I could do. My overactive and anxious mind wanted to start to worry about finals when I was still in week one of classes. I could never have made it if I would have continued to fret about the end of each semester when the semester had just begun. I had to give the worries one by one over to the Lord. He was faithful every day. There were times I had to make sacrifices. I definitely still spent quality time with my family, but I was not always able to make every single family outing.

However, I knew the temporary sacrifice would pay off. When I was close to graduating I was also close to delivering our 3rd child, Trenton. One of the requirements was I needed to travel to Virginia to complete my last one-week intensive. At the time I was eight months pregnant and looked like I was about to burst, but I knew I needed to fulfill this requirement in order to graduate. It would seem this would have caused me great anxiety but surprisingly I was able to rationally tell myself and my husband, "If I go into labor, Virginia has good hospitals as well." I knew God would take care of me and He did.

It is essential when you have come out of a season whether positive or negative that you pause and look back and recognize the faithfulness of God. He never failed me or left me. He did not let me give up on myself. However, this is where it gets confusing for some people. God will help you but He will NOT do it for you. The Bible says we are co-workers with Christ. I Corinthians 3:9 (Amplified) says, "For we are God's fellow workers [His servants working together]; you are God's cultivated field [His garden, His vineyard], God's building."

Think of yourself as being in partnership with God, because you are. It is so powerful that when we are surrendered in complete obedience to Him, He always will put His "super" on top of our "natural" and it becomes "supernatural." What an impact we can make in the Kingdom of God. It reminds me of the story I heard about the mouse and the elephant that were crossing a bridge one day. When they got to the other side, the mouse looks at his friend the elephant and proclaims, "Wow! Didn't we shake that bridge?" The elephant knowingly, but kindly replies, "Yes we did my friend."

Being in partnership with Jesus means that with Him we can shake that bridge! We can accomplish mighty exploits! We can fulfill His purpose for our life!

Decide today to take off the cloak of shame seeped in past failures and secret sins. I challenge you to find one safe person who you will take a risk with and share something the Enemy has been using against you and hanging over your head. When we open our mouth and begin to share the scariest and darkest secrets from our past, light comes in and freedom begins to illuminate our lives.

Revelation 12:11 declares, "They triumphed over him by the blood of the Lamb and by the word of their testimony; they did not love their lives so much as to shrink from death." We overcome Satan when we are no longer afraid to come out of the shadows of fear, doubt, insecurity, and shame. The Enemy cannot triumph over us when we are not ashamed to tell others what God has delivered us from and done for us.

I am not the only one with a testimony. You also have something to share that people need to hear. Dare to believe that God wants to use your voice, your words, and your life to bring healing and wholeness to many people. We cannot do it alone, but we are not alone! He has promised to never leave us or forsake us.

When the children of Israel had been wandering in the wilderness for 40 years and were finally getting ready to cross over into the Promised Land the Lord reminded them of this. Deuteronomy 31:6 says, "Be strong and courageous. Do not be afraid or terrified because of them, for the Lord your God goes with you; He will never leave you nor forsake you."

Sometimes right before your biggest breakthrough the Enemy tries one last time to bring the greatest fear and discouragement. Fight like a good, heavily armed soldier with your spiritual armor in place. Ephesians 6:10-17 is filled with what we need to wear spiritually in order to be victorious on a daily basis. Fight with your armor on and know that with the Lord on your side you can certainly possess the Promised Land and fulfill His plan and purpose for your life!

Appendix A

21 Verses for Meditation

Deuteronomy 31:8
The Lord himself goes before you and will be with you; he will never leave you nor forsake you. Do not be afraid; do not be discouraged.

Psalm 40:2-3
He lifted me out of the slimy pit, out of the mud and mire; he set my feet on a rock and gave me a firm place to stand. He put a new song in my mouth, a hymn of praise to our God. Many will see and fear and put their trust in the Lord.

Psalm 42:5
Why are you downcast, O my soul? Why so disturbed within me? Put your hope in God, for I will yet praise him, my Savior and my God.

Psalm 55:22
Cast your cares on the Lord and he will sustain you; he will never let the righteous fall.

Psalm 91:1-2
He who dwells in the shelter of the Most High will rest in the shadow of the Almighty. I will say of the Lord, "He is my refuge and my fortress, my God, in whom I trust."

Psalm 116:1
I love the Lord, for he heard my voice; he heard my cry
for mercy.

Psalm 116:8-9
For you, O Lord, have delivered my soul from death, my
eyes from tears, my feet from stumbling, that I may walk
before the Lord in the land of the living.

Psalm 121:1-4 I lift up my eyes to the hills – where does
my help come from? My help comes from the Lord, the
Maker of heaven and earth. He will not let your foot slip-
he who watches over you will not slumber; indeed, he
who watches over Israel will neither slumber nor sleep.

Psalm 130:1-2
Out of the depths I cry to you, O Lord; O Lord, hear my
voice. Let your ears be attentive to my cry for mercy.

Proverbs 3:5-6
Trust in the Lord with all your heart and lean not on your
own understanding; in all your ways acknowledge him,
and he will make your paths straight.

Isaiah 40:27-31
Why do you say, O Jacob, and complain, O Israel, "My
way is hidden from the Lord; my cause is disregarded
by my God"? Do you not know? Have you not heard?
The Lord is the everlasting God, the Creator of the ends
of the earth. He will not grow tired or weary, and his

understanding no one can fathom. He gives strength to the weary and increases the power of the weak. Even youths grow tired and weary, and young men stumble and fall; but those who hope in the Lord will renew their strength. They will soar on wings like eagles; they will run and not grow weary, they will walk and not be faint.

Isaiah 41:10, So do not fear, for I am with you; do not be dismayed, for I am your God. I will strengthen you and help you; I will uphold you with my righteous right hand.

Isaiah 43:1-2
But now, this is what the Lord says – he who created you, O Jacob, he who formed you, O Israel: "Fear not, for I have redeemed you; I have summoned you by name; you are mine. When you pass through the waters, I will be with you; and when you pass through the rivers, they will not sweep over you. When you walk through the fire, you will not be burned; the flames will not set you ablaze.

Jeremiah 29:11
For I know the plans I have for you, declares the Lord, plans to prosper you and not to harm you, plans to give you hope and a future.

Matthew 11:28-30
Come to me, all you who are weary and burdened, and I will give you rest. Take my yoke upon you and learn from me, for I am gentle and humble in heart, and you

will find rest for your souls. For my yoke is easy and my burden is light.

John 14:27
Peace I leave with you; my peace I give you. I do not give to you as the world gives. Do not let your hearts be troubled and do not be afraid.
John 16:33
I have told you these things, so that in me you may have peace. In this world you will have trouble. But take heart! I have overcome the world.

2 Corinthians 1:3-4
Praise be to the God and Father of our Lord Jesus Christ, the Father of compassion and the God of all comfort, who comforts us in all our troubles, so that we can comfort those in any trouble with the comfort we ourselves have received from God.

2 Corinthians 12:9-10
But he said to me, "My grace is sufficient for you, for my power is made perfect in weakness." Therefore I will boast all the more gladly about my weaknesses, so that Christ's power may rest on me. That is why, for Christ's sake, I delight in weaknesses, in insults, in hardships, in persecutions, in difficulties. For when I am weak, then I am strong.

Philippians 4:6-8
Do not be anxious about anything, but in everything, by

prayer and petition, with thanksgiving, present your requests to God. And the peace of God, which transcends all understanding, will guard your hearts and your minds in Christ Jesus.

Finally, brothers, whatever is true, whatever is noble, whatever is right, whatever is pure, whatever is lovely, whatever is admirable – if anything is excellent or praiseworthy – think about such things.

I Peter 5:7

Cast all your anxiety on him because he cares for you.

Appendix B

Healthy Food for a Healthy Brain

- Almonds, tree nuts
- Apples
- Asparagus
- Avocados
- Bananas
- Beans (black, garbanzo, pinto)
- Beets
- Bell peppers
- Blackberries
- Blueberries
- Broccoli
- Brussels Sprouts
- Carrots
- Cherries
- Chicken, skinless
- Cranberries
- Grapefruit
- Green tea
- Honeydew
- Kiwi
- Lemons
- Lentils
- Limes
- Oats
- Oranges, citrus fruits
- Pomegranates
- Raspberries

- Red grapes
- Spinach
- Strawberries
- Sweet potatoes and yams
- Tofu
- Tomatoes
- Tuna
- Turkey, skinless
- Walnuts
- Whole grains

Appendix C

Mental Health Resources

Christian Counselors Network
www.Focusonthefamily.com/counseling/find-a-counselor

National Alliance on Mental Illness
www.nami.org

National Institute of Mental Health
www.nimh.nih.gov

National Suicide Prevention Lifeline
1-800-273-8255 (TALK)
www.suicidepreventionlifeline.org

The National Hopeline Network
1-800-SUICIDE or 1-800-784-2433
www.hopeline.com

REFERENCES

Chapter 1: Blindsided by Bipolar Disorder

1. Morris, S.Y. (2016, November 14). Bipolar disorder psychosis. Retrieved from http://www.healthline.com/health/bipolar-disorder-psychosis

2. McGee, R.S. (1991) The Search for Significance. Houston, TX: Rapha Publishing.

Chapter 2: Coping with a Mental Diagnosis

1. Some content taken from BLUE GENES, by Paul Meier. Copyright © 2005. Used by permission of Tyndale House Publisher, Inc. All rights reserved.

Chapter 4: My Path to Healing

1. Grazer, B. (Producer), & Howard, R. (Director). (2001). A Beautiful Mind [Motion Picture]. United States: Imagine Entertainment.

2. Arterburn, S. & Felton, J. (2001). Toxic Faith. Colorado Springs, CO: WaterBrook Press.

3. Joyner, R. (2007). The Final Quest. Fort Mill, SC: Morning Star Publications.

Chapter 9: Neurotransmitters and Mental Health

1. Nemade, R. (2007, September 19). Biology of Depression-Neurotransmitters. Retrieved from http://www.mentalhelp.net

2. Dipardo, R. (2013, August 16). Glutamate & Depression. Retrieved from http://www.livestrong.com

Chapter 10: Major Depressive Disorder

1. U.S. Department of Health and Human Services, National Institutes of Health, National Institute of Mental Health. (2016, October). Depression. Retrieved from http://www.nimh.nih.gov

Chapter 11: Anxiety Disorders

1. Anxiety and Depression Association of America. Generalized Anxiety Disorder. Retrieved from http://www.adaa.org-understanding-anxiety/generalized-anxiety-disorder-gad

Chapter 14: 8 Healthy Habits for a Healthy Life

1. (n.d.). Dictionary.com Unabridged. Retrieved from Dictionary.com website http://www.dictionary.com

2. Cloud, H., & Townsend, J. (1992) Boundaries: When to say yes when to say no to take control of your life. Grand Rapids, MI: Zondervan.